Arriving
in
America

Arriving in America

Destination
The South

Patricia Ann Taylor

authorHOUSE®

AuthorHouse™
1663 Liberty Drive
Bloomington, IN 47403
www.authorhouse.com
Phone: 1-800-839-8640

Published by AuthorHouse   11/11/2014

ISBN: 978-1-4918-5382-5 (sc)
ISBN: 978-1-4918-5384-9 (hc)
ISBN: 978-1-4918-5383-2 (e)

Library of Congress Control Number: 2014901005

To my daughters Tracie Marie Denise Hawkins-Gaines, Dawn Millette Mopkins, Taylor Ashley Jackson and beloved son William Don Mopkins, Jr. this is your legacy, my personal gift to you.

TABLE OF CONTENTS

INTRODUCTION

My passion for family history began when I saw the movie Roots, years ago. I did not want a collection of names, places and dates in my genealogical research. My passion became so strong that my desire was to incorporate The Total Black Experience – from parts of Africa (mainly West Africa) through American slavery, The Black Migration to the southern states of Louisiana and Mississippi. This passionate journey has resulted in me writing this book.

In my research, I discovered and learned many things about my family history along with American history. I discovered blood ties between my ancestors and people of European and/or Indian descent; family members (brothers) separated during slavery and scattered throughout the states of Georgia, Mississippi and Louisiana; family members who fought in the Civil War; life threatening epidemics that caused the life of so many people including members of my family; and a seventh generation great grandmother, uncovering how her descendent were passed down within one slave-owning family.

My research includes travel to North, South, East and West Africa. This includes Accra, Ghana; Nairobi, Kenya; Senegal (Dakar, Banjul); South Africa (Soweto, Pretoria and Johannesburg); Harare, Zimbabwe; Benin; The Gambia; Tanzania and Cairo, Egypt. My travels throughout West Africa enabled me to connect with various ethnic groups, such as Mandinkas, Senegalese and Kenyans. Traveling from the United States these ethnic groups welcomed me and called me their "sister". My tours of the El Mina Castle in Ghana and Point of No Return in Benin, brought water to my eyes imagining what my ancestors and other Africans went through, as they passed through this exit, never to return to their homeland again. Inside the El Mina Castle I saw dungeons where male, female and children were held upon captivity. The Africans had been captured, and brought there to wait for ships to take them to America. I also toured the Village of Juffure, where author, Alex Haley found his "roots" in the Gambia.

My travels also included Charleston, South Carolina; Woodville, Mississippi; Plaquemine, Louisiana; Raleigh-Durham, North Carolina; Atlanta, Georgia; Memphis, Tennessee; Birmingham, Alabama; Betheseda, Maryland; Indianapolis, Indiana; New York City; Cincinnati, Ohio; and Louisville, Kentucky. My visits to these regions provided a wealth of information through various museums, plantations and on site places of interest. It was almost like walking in the footsteps of my ancestors.

The sources for this book was taken from authentic and authoritative genealogy sources that contained information about the Taylor, Martin, Asberry, Gay, Netterville, Gay and Veal families. My interest focuses on the arrival of Africans to America and their migration to the south, particularly focusing on my descendent. This book provides names, relationships, occupations, military service, pictures and more about these families, with a focus mostly on the period from 1800-1900. The information on surname matches of my ancestors and named slave holders is intended to provide data for consideration by those seeking to make connections between slaveholders and former slaves.

Hopefully, this book will leave the reader with a burning desire to begin their on journey. Tools that I found useful were state censuses, death and marriage certificates, records of southern plantations, and oral interviews from family members. In search of my ancestry roots, I was confronted with many obstacles. I discovered that tracing an ancestor brought to America in chains requires an extensive search, if records could be located, for many records are gone forever. This book is my legacy to my children. I felt obligated to research and document the history of my family a best as I could because I wished that when I was at a tender age, I had asked questions to family members who are now deceased. I want future generations from my family to know from whence they came.

THE GREAT MIGRATION

To escape the uncertainty of the political and religion uncertainty found in England, many English families boarded ships at a great expense to sail for the colonies held by Britain. The passages were expensive, though, and the boats were unsafe, overcrowded, and ridden with disease. Those who were lucky enough to make the passage intact were rewarded with land, opportunity, and social environment less prone to religious and political persecution. Many of these families went on to be important contributors to the young nation, the United States where they settled. The Nettervilles and Gays were among some of the immigrants to arrive in North America from England.

Slavery had existed for hundreds of years. The Book of Exodus speaks about how the people of Israel were enslaved by the Romans. Webster defines a slave as "one that is completely subservient to a dominating influence". The demand for slave labor in the new nation led to trade in Africa that was through purchase or warfare and raids. European merchandise such as weapons, gun powder and rum were imported into Africa in exchange for slaves. There were many tribes across the continent of Africa. The close proximity of the settlements to the sea, offered very little safety from raids for slaves by European slave traders who would navigate their ships to the shores of the ocean for their human cargo. The purchased or captured slaves were placed in forts that served temporarily as prisons until the slave ship (vessel) reached its quota.

The Bambaras tribe lived within the inland part of Africa (Niger). They probably were one of the tribes that was captured in warfare with other tribes and shipped out of Senegalese ports. The Bambaras are described "tall and slender build, with fine features and a fuller beard". The Fula tribe was tall, lightly built people. The Wolof tribes who are of Fula origin also tend to be tall. My Taylor ancestors, Joseph William (1904) and his father William "Willie" (1878) were tall in stature. Living in the swamps of Louisiana, as strong, tall men they worked as swampers (lumbermen), cutting timber. Could they have been descendent of the Wolof, Fula or Bambaras tribes? The "Pgymies" is sometimes

A map illustrating contemporary Africa, denoting the areas where the Fula, Mandinka, Wolof, Bambaras and Bambuto people have occupied for centuries.

Map of contemporary Africa, denoting the areas where the Mandinka, Fula and other peoples have occupied for centuries

used to refer to a group of people found in Central Africa. Many were short in stature. My Asberry ancestors were often described as short in stature. A World War I Draft registration dated 1918 show William Asberry (1895), my great great grandfather was short. My grandmother, Hattie Beatrice was approximately 4 feet 11. She was called "shorty". Could my Asberry family be descendent of the Pygmies tribe?

The exact African origin of slaves in Louisiana and Mississippi cannot be traced with any accuracy. The French largely controlled the Senegal region in Africa. It is possible that a great number of Africans in the French colonies were Senegalese, sailing from a Senegalese port. Some of the tribes near the Gambia River included the Wolof, Mandinka, Fulani, Fula, Serer, Jola and Manjago tribes. Ghana is the country which is called The Gold Coast. Some of the tribes neat The Gold Coast were the Ashanti, Fanti, Ewe, Guan, Gurma, Ga-Adangbe, Mole-Dagbani, Luba-Mossi, Guro, Songhye, Fang, Baule, Dan, Bambara, Bete, Choku, Youre and Senufo tribes.

On July 28, 1998 I visited El Mina Castle in Ghana. As a fort, El Mina was holding slaves until they were ready for the Atlantic voyage. It was accessible to slave-carrying ships. There were quarters for merchants and traders; and there were dark dungeons where slaves were kept. There was also a courtyard for the branding of slaves. Men, women and children were kept in separate dungeons. I also saw an area where slaves exited for awaiting ships. Some of these slave ships (vessels) were The Aurora, La Amistad, Brookes, Clotide (the last reported ship to U. S. 1859-1860), Desire, Duc du Maine, Hope, Lord Ligonier, Wanderer and Zong. Other well- known slave forts were Cape Coast Castle, Cormantine and Goree.

Our nation was built on the backs of slavery. People like the Dutch and other Europeans went to the coasts of Africa where Africans were brought and captured to bring to this nation, for profit. In their minds, Africans were an inferior group and was most useful in servitude. Many men, women and children were taken from their homeland, despite their cry out. The ship was overcrowded. They were shackled with smells of stench. They were washed down like animals with buckets of water poured over them. Many could not communicate with each other. Their journey was long. Some committed suicide by themselves overboard into the Atlantic Ocean. Their travel from the coast of Maryland and Virginia were over thousands of miles. The African man, woman and child were in a foreign land, shackled and scared, sold to the highest bidder. They probably missed and longed for the families that they left in Africa. The Africans were sold like property. They could no longer identify with their homeland. They lost the use of their African names, language and customs. I descended from one of these tribes. Their new names were Taylor, Martin, Veal, Gay, Asberry, Jones and Netterville.

The Great Migration, was not from Africa, but from the Thirteen Colonies to the southern states. The Thirteen Colonies were Virginia, Massachusetts, Maryland, New Hampshire, Connecticut, Rhode Island, Delaware, Georgia, Pennsylvania, North Carolina, South Carolina, New York and New Jersey. Residents of the Thirteen Colonies were mostly independent farmers who owned their own land and voted for their local government. In the 1760's and 1770's the colonies united militarily in opposition to Great Britain with the outbreak of the Revolutionary War in 1775. In 1776, they declared independence and formed a new nation, THE UNITED STATES OF AMERICA.

Millions of enslaved Africans were moved south and west from Maryland, Virginia, North Carolina and South Carolina to Georgia, Mississippi, Louisiana, Texas and elsewhere. Commonly used slaves routes were:

A map illustrating various routes possibly taken by my ancestors migrating to Louisiana and Mississippi from Wheeling, West Virginia; Richmond, Virginia; Maryland; Charleston, South Carolina; Georgia and Tennessee.

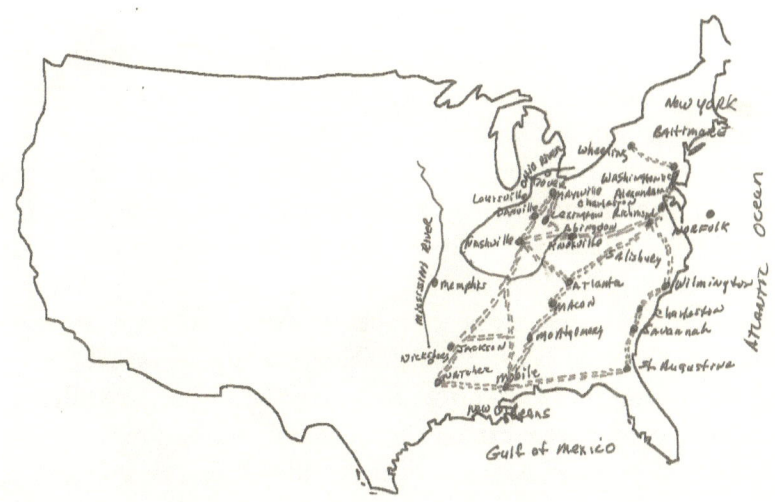

**A map illustrating various routes taken by African
AMERICANS MIGRATING TO Southern States.**

The Baltimore to Wheeling Corridor, which fed Ohio River interior slave markets from Charleston, Virginia to Maysville and Louisville, Kentucky and on to the Mississippi River and St. Louis, Missouri. The Tidewater Corridor which linked Richmond and Arlington, Virginia with Alexandria and Danville, Kentucky through the Cumberland Gap. The Southern Appalachian Corridor, which ran south from Norfolk, Virginia through Salisbury, North Carolina to the markets in Charleston, South Carolina. The Southwestern Appalachian Corridor which led from Lexington, Kentucky through Louisville, Nashville, Tennessee and down the Natchez trail to Mississippi.

My ancestors could have traveled anyone or all of these routes. Based upon my research, I highly suspect that my ancestors – the Gay, Veal and Jones (Johns) may have been moved from Maryland and Virginia by their slaveholder using the Baltimore to Wheeling Corridor destination to Mississippi. My Taylor, Martin and Asberry ancestor slaveholder possibly used the Southern Appalachian Corridor – North Carolina and South Carolina markets to Louisiana.

Slavery in New York began during the 1600's when the Dutch West India Company brought African slaves to the New Amsterdam Colony. England seized New Amsterdam in 1664 and renamed it New York. Slavery continued under British rule. As stated earlier, most of the slaves came from West Central Africa. Universal emancipation for all slaves in

New York was achieved in 1827. As the civil war approached, the south became identified with slavery, and the north with free labor. In May 1991, three hundred years of silence was shattered with the discovery of the African Burial Ground in lower Manhattan. Following public outcry, at least four hundred burials was unearth that provided valuable information about the slaves health, diet, gender, age, physical condition and cause of death. In 1993, The African Burial Ground was designated National Historic Landmark.

Life for slaves was difficult. They worked from sun up to sun down. As slaves, they worked as field laborers, carpenters and domestic servants. If rebellion took place, they were beaten or sold. Research indicates that they were exposed to malnutrition, backbreaking labor and recurrent illnesses. Many African families were torn apart. In May 2014, I visited Farmington Plantation and found upon entering the grounds a memorial that read "In memory of the enslaved African Americans at Farmington". A letter written by Abraham Lincoln in 1841 following a visit to Farmington Plantation explains in great detail how difficult life was for slaves. In 1841, Farmington Plantation was owned by Joshua and Mary Speed in Louisville, Kentucky. The Speeds owned at least 62 slaves. In the letter, Lincoln wrote about his encounter with enslaved Africans aboard the steamboat trip home to Springfield, "a fine example was presented on board the boast for contemplating the effect of human happiness. A gentleman had purchased twelve Negroes in different parts of Kentucky and was taking them to a farm in the south. They were chained six and six together. A small iron clevis was around the left wrist of each, and this fastened to the main chain by a shorter one at a convenient distance from, the others; so that the Negroes were strung together precisely like so many fish upon a trout-line. In this condition they were being separated forever from the scenes of their childhood, their friends, their fathers and mothers, and brothers and sisters, and many of them from wives and children, and going into perpetual slavery where the lash of the master is proverbially more ruthless and unrelenting than any other".

The 13th Amendment, The Emancipation with the civil war abolished slavery in December 1865. Many of the people were enslaved participated in the civil war. Upon the end of slavery, Reconstruction began. The Africans need ways and means to make a living. The Freedom Bureau and the Maryland Union Commission were established to assist with food, housing and transportation. Maryland thought that it was the best for the most Blacks to be transported south. Migrating from Maryland, Virginia, Georgia, North Carolina, South Carolina, my ancestors now found themselves living in the towns of Woodville, Mississippi and Plaquemine, Louisiana.

A question that may come to mind is how did the enslaved people from Maryland, Virginia, Tennessee, North Carolina, South Carolina and Georgia arrive in Mississippi and Louisiana. The answer may be the "new slaveholder" who purchased him/her. One mode of transportation used was the steamboat. The Edward James Steamboat was built in 1869. This steamboat and others like it carried thousands of bales of cotton and passengers (slaves for cheap labor) making their owners rich. My ancestors, Nancy Jones, Patsey Martin, Isaac Asberry, William Veal, Mary Veal and Joe Netterville as slaves, provided labor making their owners prosperous and rich.

Perhaps my ancestor, Nancy Jones aka "Unice" born about 1815 and died 1813, is one of the Africans that was taken from her tribe an brought to the New Nation. The 1880 census under "place of birth" column for mother and father was blank. What does this mean? Could Nancy's parents been descendent of Africa/ Was "Unice" Nancy's African name/ Her children are listed on the 1870 census with the names of Sarre, Peyton and Armlia. Could those be African names? Was the name "Nancy Johns" given to her by her slaveholder and the surname "Jones" changed following her emancipation?

Isreal taylor was born about 1827 and his wife Affay Taylor born about 1829 in North Carolina. Official documents show Isreal's parents were from Virginia and Maryland. What tribes in Africa did Isreal's parents derive from when the docked on the ports of Virginia and Maryland? Was Affay also one of the Africans who arrive in North Carolina and later sold by her owner to a Louisiana slaveholder where she met Isreal? The answers to these questions will forever be unknown.

William Martin born about 1812 in Maryland and his wife Patsey Martin was born about 1815 in Virginia. Could they have been born at an earlier date? Are they too possibly Africans who were stolen or sold by their own "people" into slavery in exchange for weapons, gun powder and rum? Watching the movie "Twelve Years of Slavery" produced by Steve McQueen, based upon a true story brought a sharp pain to my heart. One of the characters, "Patsey" was sexually exploited by her master and because of jealously by his wife, "Patsey" was punished and severely beaten with multiple lashes for leaving the plantation to go to a neighboring plantation for a bar of soap. This scene was particularly unbearable because my ancestor "Patsey" was born about 1815 (around the same period as the character in the movie) in Virginia and later found herself also in Louisiana, where the movie, a true story, took place (St. Mary Parish).

Isaac Asberry was born about 1820 and his wife Julia Asberry was born about 1820. Both are from Virginia. Are they too Africans that was given the names of Isaac and Julia by their Virginia slaveholder? My Asberry ancestors are known for having short statues. Could this be a clue to what region or tribe they might have derived from in Africa?

William Veal was born about 1802 and died 1885. His brother, Robert Veal, Sr. was born about 1807 and died 1895. Official documents show their place of birth is Tennessee. William married Mary (dob 1819-1890) of Maryland. Robert married Maria (dob 1820-1900) of Georgia. This family, according to dates of birth may have been Africans that found themselves on a crowded ship with other tribes, scared and unable to communicate with the African lying next to him or her because of language. Many questions will forever be unknown. How did the brothers who once lived in Tennessee meet their wives who lived in Maryland and Georgia? Did the Tennessee slaveholder sell one brother to a Maryland slaveholder and the other to a Georgia slaveholder? Official documents shows William's third known child, Mary Veal (my great great great grandmother) was born in Maryland in 1838, so he had already migrated from Tennessee to Maryland. The 1880 census shows the brothers, William and Robert, had migrated to Woodville, Mississippi. There is information that my Veal ancestors had already migrated to Mississippi before the Emancipation Proclamation in 1863. Mary Veal's son, my great great grandfather, Anthony Gay was born in 1857 in Mississippi. It is highly unlikely that my Veal ancestors moved from Maryland voluntarily as during this period they were enslaved. Did the Maryland slaveholder sell William Veal to a Mississippi slaveholder or did the slaveholder himself migrate to the Mississippi region taking slaves with him? These questions will forever be unanswered, too. Mary Veal (dob 1836) may not have been born in Africa but her mother Mary Veal (dob 1819) most likely had to endure that long journey across the Atlantic that mostly took months.

There was some interbreeding between Africans, with the Indians and with the Europeans. A new race of American Blacks was created, a race with the blood of many tribes and many nations in its veins. Sophia Gay, my great great great grandmother (dob 1863) often talked about having Indian in her bloodline. Sophia's mother was born in 1815. Sophia's children had features of light-skinned, straight nose and hair. Pictures of her nieces, distinctively shows evidence of interbreeding.

There were twenty-one known Indian tribes in the area of present day Mississippi between the years 1500 and 1800. The focus here will be on Indian tribes reported during the late 1700s when the conflicts, alliances and cultural dissolutions of most tribes reached their peak. Regional boundaries of the State of Mississippi did not exist during the period of time represented for these tribes. Streams and rivers were generally associated with tribal locations. Some of the tribes included the Acolopissa, meaning "those who listen and see"; the Chickasaw, meaning "to sit", was a large, strong, war-like tribe, they continuously fighting with adjacent tribes as well as the French. As a tribe, they were ever defeated and only by treaty in 1832 did they give up their Mississippi lands and move to Indian Territory in Oklahoma between 1837 and 1847; the Choctaw were one of the largest tribes in Southeast Mississippi, the meaning of their name is unclear; the Houma, meaning "red". They plaited their hair and tattooed their faces. The Homochitto national Forest is nearby Wilkinson County where my Veal and Gay ancestors called home. Could my great great great grandmother, Sophia Gay bloodline be linked to the Homochitto Indian tribe? The Natchez were one of the best known tribes in Mississippi due to French settlement in their territory. Other tribes included the Choula/Chula, Griga, Ibitoupa, Koroa, Tunica, Tiou, Taposa,Ofo/Ofogoula?Mosoplia, Pascagoula, Pensacola, Quapaw, Yazoo, Sawokli/Sabougla/Samboukia, Taposa, Tiou, and Tunica tribe.

In Mississippi, the Natchez area was the first Mississippi region where plantations were established. African slaves were introduced into the Mississippi plantation system in the early 1700s by French colonists. Tobacco was the first major crop that thrived from African slave labor. The invention of the cotton gin by Eli Whitney allowed the European planter to greatly increase their wealth via the production of cotton. The plantation system involved the planter living in an elegant home far from the farm land. The planter hired overseers to live on and manage the plantations. African-slave labor was used by large-scale and small farms. After the civil war, many newly "freed" American-born Africans worked in the pine forests cutting trees for lumber and turpentine (see Taylor section).

Woodville, Mississippi, where my Veal and Gay ancestors called home is located on Highway 61 about halfway between Natchez and St. Francisville, Louisiana. It is about 130 miles from New Orleans, Louisiana. Woodville was first settled near the turn of the nineteenth century and was incorporated as a town in 1811. The county seat, Wilkinson was named after a Commander-in-Chief of the Unit4ed States Army, General James Wilkinson. It is reported that the first African slaves were brought to Wilkinson County prior to 1790 and were settled in the western part of the county. Many slaves from Wilkinson County fought for the Confederate Army during the civil war. My research found my ancestor Robert Veal was enlisted in The United States Colored troops on February 16, 1864 in Natchez, Mississippi at age 18 years old. The document lists him as "deserted". I wonder if the desertion was because he did not want to fight such a war for the Confederacy (see Veal section).

Throughout various regions, Mississippi had many slave workplaces (plantations). In Wilkinson County, the two plantations that are of interest with a possible link to my Veal and Gay ancestors are The Bowling Green Plantation located in Woodville, and the Cliffwood Plantation, located in Pinckneyville, Mississippi. During this period, the Cliffwood Plantation is associated with a possible slaveholder named John Burruss. Mr. Burruss was a Methodist minister of Virginia and planter of Woodville and Cliffwood Plantations. The Bowling Green Plantation is associated with a possible slaveholder named Edward McGhee. A family of slaves, the Veal family is associated with the McGehee's. My great great uncle, Edward James Gay was married to Patsy Gay. According to official documents, Patsy Gay was born in 1889 and died April 1970 in Pinckneyville, Mississippi (this is the same area where The Cliffwood Plantation was once owned by John Burruss).

Judge Edward McGehee was born in 1786. He died around 1880. Judge McGehee was a native of Georgia. Around 1807, at the age of 21, his father, Micajah McGehee gave him money to buy slaves and supplies. Edward went to Wheeling, West Virginia where he bought a horse, a flat boat, his slaves and other supplies. He put everything on the flatboat and headed down the Ohio River and then down the Mississippi. Edward landed at Fort Adams, a region in the Mississippi territory (nearby Woodville). He bought land that was known as Thompson's Creek. In 1831, increasingly wealthy, Edward McGehee built a three story mansion, and called it Bowling Green. The Bowling Green Plantation Home was burned October 1864 by a troop of Northern soldiers.

During this period (1800 – 1900) which I have titled "The Great Migration", my ancestors witnessed the terms of several United States Presidents. They include – President James Monroe (1817-1825); President John Quincy Adams (1825-1829); President Andrew Jackson (1829-1837); President Martin Van Buren (1837-1841); President William Henry Harrison (1841); President John Tyler (1841-1845); President James Polk (1845-1849); President Zachary Taylor (1849-1850); and President Benjamin Harrison (1889-1893) who is known as the centennial president, inaugurated 100 years after George Washington. He is also the grandson of our 9th president – President William Henry Harrison.

The African Burial National Monument located in Manhattan, New York and is widely regarded as one of America's most significant archeological finds of the 20th century.

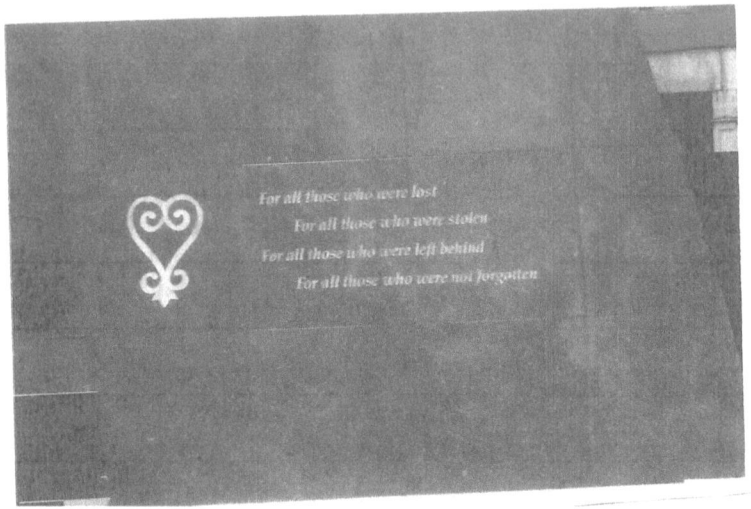

The heart-like Sankofa from West Africa means
"learn from the past to prepare for the future".

Ships similar to this Dutch vessel carried enslaved
Africans to British North America.

This is a picture of the Ohio River; the bridge is the Sherman
Minton Bridge which connects Kentucky to Indiana. Crossing
this river by many that were enslaved meant Freedom.

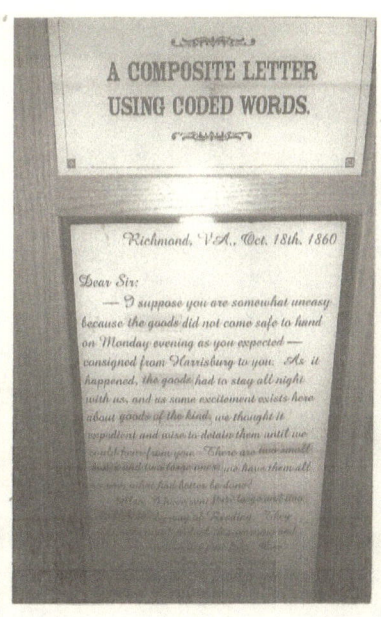
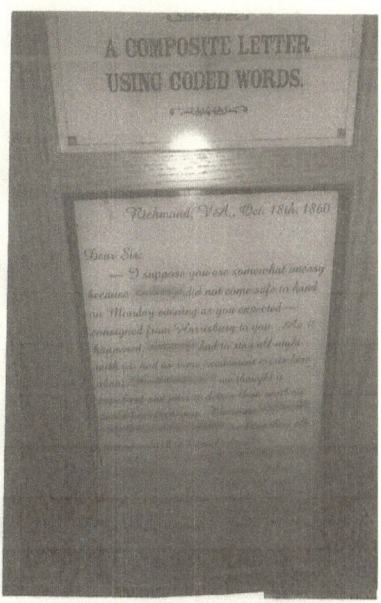

An example of a coded letter used to help runaways
through The Underground Railroad.

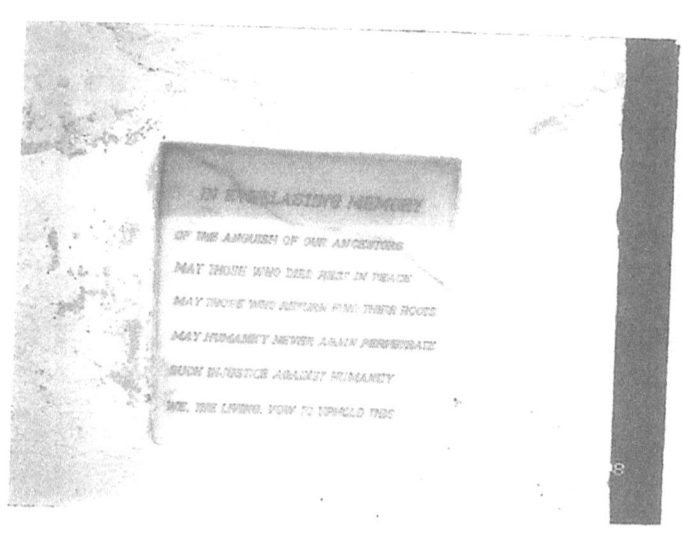

In August 1998, my husband and I toured The Elmina Castle. A memorial sign is placed outside the castle to remind those that enter that NEVER AGAIN should humanity penetrate such injustice.

Pictured with children of Benin; their official language is French.

In a West African village; I have no idea what I
am doing or making, I think it is bread.

Statute of an African couple found in the
Village of Juffure, The Gambia.

Pictured with a Senegalese Woman.

A West African Village.

Pictured with a Mandinka girl in the Gambia.

Here I am at the Maison des Esclaves, the slave house at
Goree Island listening to the tour guide tell the group about
the inhumanity and brutality the African captives faced
whilw housed here before their departure from Africa.

"The Door of No Return" where millions of Africans made their last footsteps, as they marched through that door in chains never to return to their homeland. Imagining what my ancestors and other Africans went through as they passed through this exit, the pictured smile you see later turned to tears.

VEAL/GAY

A question that always came up was how did William Veal and Robert Veal, two brothers from Tennessee find and eventually marry their brides, Mary from Virginia and Maria from Georgia? The answer to this question could be due to slaveholders, Edward McGehee and Duncan Stewart, who eventually migrated with their slaves to Woodville, Mississippi. The McGhees had originally emigrated from Scotland to Virginia. They later migrated to Georgia and then moved westward to Alabama, and then Mississippi. Research shows that the Veal slave families of Georgia, and Mississippi is linked to the McGhee/Stewart families.

Duncan Stewart, a politician was a native of Bladen County, North Carolina. Duncan was born about 1763 and died in 1820. Duncan's father owned slaves in North Carolina. Duncan Stewart served in the North Carolina legislature and senate. Duncan and his family moved to the Tennessee Territory in 1794 and he served in the legislature and senate in the state of Tennessee. He was a surveyor and a land dealer in Tennessee. Duncan Stewart and his family moved around 1809 to the Mississippi Territory. They probably brought slaves with them from Tennessee to Woodville, Mississippi (see map 1-2). An 1880 census shows my ancestor, William Veal was born about 1802 and his place of birth is Tennessee. Duncan Stewart served in the Territory Legislature and became the Lt. Governor of the state of Mississippi. When Duncan Stewart died in 1820 he owned 65 slaves. Holly Grove Plantation in Wilkinson County was begun by Duncan Stewart. In the 1860 census there were 346 slaves listed. My research found that a "William Veal and Henderson Veal" contracted as freedmen to work on Holly Grove after the civil war. It is the William Veal from Holly Grove that was supposedly the same William Veal in "So Red the Rose", a novel by Stark Young. In this book, the Bowling Green Plantation is called Montrose. This novel portrays southern culture combined with one's family history. The novel was made into a movie and produced by Paramount Pictures in 1935 (4 years before Gone with the Wind). In the movie, supposedly William Veal was patterned on a Stewart butler. In my ancestry search, I found that my ancestor William Veal (1880 census) shows his occupation as a house servant (butler). It should also be noted that a 1940 census shows William Veal's grandson, Preston Veal (dob 1876) a native of Woodville, Mississippi graduated from college.

The McGehee and Stewart families were tied through marriage. Judge Edward McGehee's son John Burruss McGehee married Catherine Stewart, Duncan Stewart's granddaughter. Also, their siblings married. Caroline McGehee married Duncan Stewart (grandson of Duncan Stewart). John and Catherine's son was named James Stewart McGhee. Catherine's parents were James Alexander Stewart and Julianna Randolph Stewart. Both families lived at laurel hill near each other on land given to them by Judge Edward McGehee. John and Catherine Stewart lived at Woodlawn Plantation. Laurel Hill was located in West Feliciana Parish in Louisiana. The Stewart family was also connected to other plantations in West Feliciana, Point Coupee, East and West Baton Rouge, Terrebone and Iberville Parishes in the state of Louisiana. My godfather was named Clarence Stewart (dob 1904) in Iberville Parish. His mother was named Catherine Stewart (dob 1878). Clarence's father was named James Stewart (dob 1874). A 1920 census shows Catherine's mother was born in Virginia and most likely was enslaved at birth. Could there be a possible link to the European Stewarts and my godfather's descendent? My godfather, Clarence Stewart was married to Mary Stewart (dob 1902). As a young girl, I recall being told that my godmother was a full blooded Indian. My research shows that Mary migrated from Arizona. It is unknown as to what tribe Mary may have come from, possibly Apache. Mary was petite, her skin color is what I describe as "cinnamon", with long straight hair. A known Apache is Geronimo. Other known Apaches are Cochise, Crazy Horse and Sitting Bull. The Apache is one of the last tribes to hold out against the White man regarding their territory.

Duncan Stewart and Edward McGehee family were important contributors to the United States where they settled. Edward McGehee was a successful planter. He owned 29,800 acres of land and 825 slaves. His estate before the civil war has been conservatively placed at

$2,717,000. Edward McGehee was about 78 years old when Bowling Green Plantation was burned down by Union Troops, giving the McGehee family living in the home, minutes to get out before the structure was burned down.

Simon Gay (dob 1835), my great great great grandfather was born in Liberty, Bedford County, Virginia. Very little is known about Simon Gay. Simon, born into slavery and spending most of his life enslaved, he most likely used his slaveholder's surname, which is Gay. A European, John Henderson Gay (dob 1787) was born in Rockbridge, Virginia. This is where things get interesting !!!! John had a son named Edward James Gay (dob 1833), who was also born in Liberty, Bedford County, Virginia. Could my great great great grandfather derived the surname of "Gay" from this European family? Other similarities were found in these two families, in regards to names used with future generations. Simon married Mary Veal (dob 1836) who is believed to have been born in Maryland. Mary's parents were William (dob 1802) and Mary (dob 1819) Veal. Simon and Mary bore two known children into slavery – Mary (dob 1855) and Anthony Gay (dob 1857) my great great grandfather. Mary (dob 1855) married Richard Johnson (dob 1844) about 1875. Richard and Mary had ten children. In 1900, nine of those children were still living, according to census records. The children were Frank Johnson (dob1875); Walter Johnson (dob 1877); Peter Johnson (dob 1879); Nolan Johnson (dob 1885); Mary (Nell)Johnson (dob 1888); Millie Johnson (dob 1889); William (Willie) Johnson (1894); and Mattie Johnson (dob 1896). An 1870 census shows Mary Veal Gay, a widow. Further research indicates that a Pvt. S. C. Gay died June 10, 1863 in Vicksburg, Warren County, Mississippi which is the period during the civil war. An 1880 census shows Mary Veal Gay's household members were her son Anthony Gay, age 20 and Ollie Veal, her niece age 22 years old. It is believed that Mary Veal Gay date of death was in 1911, at the age of 79 years old in Mississippi.

Could my great great great grandfather Simon Gay been a casuality of the civil war? A war that cost the lives of so many. The United States Congress passed the Second Confiscation Act in July 1862. It freed slaves of owners in rebellion against the United States. A militia act empowered the President to use freed slaves in any capacity in the army. President Lincoln was concerned with public opinion in the few states that remained in the Union as they had numerous slaveholders, as well as with Northern Democrats who supported the war but were less supportive of abolition than many Northern Republicans. In 1862, Union Army setbacks in battles led Lincoln to emancipating slaves in all states at war with the Union. In September 1862 Lincoln issued his preliminary Emancipation Proclamation announcing that all slaves in rebellious states would be free as of January 1, 1863. Another relative, Robert Veal who was only 18 years old was assigned to the Company of U. S. Colored Heavy Artillery. The United States Colored Troops (USCT) was regiments of the United States Army during the American Civil War that was composed of African American ("colored") soldiers. The USCT were first recruited in 1863, by the end of the civil war, they constituted approximately one-tenth of the Union Army.

In researching my family history/timeline it was both frustrating and exciting. I found very little information on the parents of Mary Veal Gay, who are William and Mary Veal. Born in 1802 and 1820, indicates that their parents were most likely descendent directly from Africa. Unfortunately, which region/tribe in Africa will forever be unknown. The 1870 census shows William and Mary Veal home was in Woodville, Wilkinson County, Mississippi. The family members listed in the were Kitty Veal (dob 1840); Nolan Veal (dob 1848); Charlotte Veal (dob 1851); Preston Veal (dob 1853); Florence Veal (1854); and Alvira Veal (1855). Their other children that was not listed in this census possibly because they were married or moved out were William Veal (dob 1820); Robert Veal (dob 1826); Mary Veal Gay (dob 1836); and Duncan Veal (dob 1838).

William's son Robert (dob 1826) married Virginia Veal (dob 1849). They had eleven known children – Richmond Veal 9dob 1864); Jim Veal (dob 1870); Tamar Veal (dob 1872); Emily Veal (1874); Lydia Veal (dob 1878); Willie Veal (dob 1884); Edward Veal (dob 1882); Ida Veal (dob 1887); Ella Veal (dob 1889); Mamie Veal (dob 1896); and Ollie Veal born about 1855 who was mostly likely Robert's child.

Another son, Duncan (dob 1838) married a Mary Veal (dob 1849). Their children were Milly Veal (dob 1867); twins, Nannie and Norah Veal (dob 1871) and Azarene Veal (dob 1896).

Willam Veal had a brother named Robert Veal (dob 1807-1895) also born in Tennessee. Robert Veal, Sr. married Maria Anderson Veal (dob 1820-1900). It is unclear if Maria was born in Virginia and later migrated to Georgia. The 1880 census shows her mother's "place of birth" was Africa. The 1870 census shows their children are Robert, Veal Jr. (dob 1844); Rebecca Veal (dob 1845); Jane Veal Bethley (dob 1846-1925); Clarissa Veal (1848-May 30, 1914); Benjamin Veal (dob 1849-1925); Henderson Veal (dob 1852) who might be the same Henderson Veal who contracted as freedman to work on the Holly Grove Plantation in Woodville, Wilkinson County following the civil war with his uncle, William Veal; and Isom Veal (dob 1854-1935). Other members of the household are grandchildren Sherrod Veal Scott (dob 1860); Cornelius Veal Commodore (dob 1866); Duncan Veal Commodore (dob 1869) Jonah Veal (dob 1870); and Isom Veal (dob 1870). Official documents provided me with additional information regarding this branch of the Veal family. Henderson married Silvia Veal and they had two known children, Elijah and Mishal. Clarissa married a Dunbar. Her known children are John, Becky and Dennis Dunbar. Jane married Orpheus Bethley who was from Georgia. Their two sons are Isom (dob 1870) and Nolan (dob 1871). At some point, Benjamin was a single parent and living alone with his two sons Robert and Walton. This is another documentation that further strengthen my analysis that there are blood ties between The Veal families from Mississippi and Georgia, two brothers, William and Robert born in Tennessee and later separated – one to Maryland the other to Georgia and much later both calling Woodville, Wilkinson County their home. With this information I discovered a possible link to myself and a very close friend, Darryl Cornell Veal. His blood ties is linked to the Georgia Veal and mine, the Maryland.

Simon and Mary Gay's son, Anthony married Sophia Taylor on February 16, 1882. They had five known children – William Gay (dob 1879); Annie Gay Taylor (1881); Edward James Gay (dob 1884); Clara Gay Scott (dob 1885); and Lucile Gay (dob 1886) my great grandmother. Anthony had several known other children. John Gay (dob 1880); Lizzie Gay (dob 1878); Tamar Gay (dob 1882); and Rosa Gay (dob 1883). Anthony Gay's burial site is at Cedar Rest Cemetery in Woodville, Wilkinson County, Mississippi. He died November, 1943. The mother of Anthony's children Lizzie, Tamar and Rosa is believed to be Mimah Kellogg (dob 1864) who is the niece of Sophia (the mother to his other children). Sophia is also the younger sister of Mimah's mother, Burnetta Netterville Richardson (dob 1844). Mimah Kellogg's father's name is unknown. The 1880 census lists Mimah's race as "mulatto". In an oral interview it was reported by Clara Gay Scott to her granddaughter that they had "white" brothers and sisters. This granddaughter also remembers her grandmother often referring to the "Kellogg" name, in particular a Chauncey Kellogg. For this reason, I began to do some research on this person and a little history of the Kellogg surname.

A Draft Registration Card on Chauncey E. Kellogg noted that his race was "Black", and the color of his eyes "Blue". He was born December 2, 1888 and died November 21, 1954. In further researching, the name "Kellogg" is most known for Kellogg Cornflakes Cereal. In my research of the Kellogg surname, specifically in Woodville, Wilkinson County Mississippi, in an 1880 census I found a Frances Kellogg, a mulatto born about 1840. Other family members were her five children ages 15, 11, 8, 7, and 2 years old. Frances occupation was washerwoman. Her father's "place of birth" was shown as NEW YORK, her mother's as Mississippi. In this same 1880 census, the "head of household" was listed as John Chandler, age 75 years old, born about 1805 in TENNESSEE, and "marital status" as widower. His "race" is listed as White. Frances' children father's name was not listed but the father's place of birth was listed as TENNESSEE.

Further research on the Kellogg surname told me that our nation's history tells us that slaves usually took the surname of their slaveholder. John Harvey Kellogg (February 26, 1852 – December 14, 1943) was an American medical doctor born in Battle Creek, Michigan. He ran a sanitarium using holistic methods, with a focus on nutrition, enemas and exercises. He is best known for the invention of the cornflakes breakfast cereal with his brother, Will Keith Kellogg. The idea for corn flakes began by accident when Kellogg and his younger brother, Will Keith Kellogg, left some cooked wheat to sit while they attended to some pressing matters at the sanitarium. When they returned, they found that the wheat had gone stale, but being on a strict budget, they decided to continue to process it by forcing it through rollers, hoping to obtain long sheets of dough. To their surprise, what they found instead were flakes, which they toasted and served to their patients. This event occurred on August 8, 1894, and a patent for "flaked cereals and process of preparing same" was filed on May 31, 1895, and issued on April 14, 1896. John Kellogg's parents are John Preston Kellogg (1806-1881) and Ann Janette Stanley (1824-1893). John Harvey Kellogg attended NEW

YORK University Medical College at Bellevue Hospital and graduated in 1875. He married Ella Ervilla Eaton (1853-1920) of New York, on February 22, 1879. Their marriage was more of a partnership than a marriage. John Harvey Kellogg believed that sex bred evil diseases, especially in men. He was determined to live a celibate life, and the two maintained separate bedrooms through their marriage. They did not have any biological children, but were foster parents to 42 children, legally adopting seven of them, before Ella died in 1920. John was outspoken on his belief on race and segregation though he himself raised several Black foster children. In 1906, with Irving Fisher and Charles Davenport, Kellogg founded the Race betterment Foundation which became a major center of the new movement in America. John was in favor of racial segregation and believed that immigrants and non-whites would damage the gene pool. He died in 1943, and is buried in Oak Hill Cemetery Battle Creek, Michigan, along with his parents, C. W. Post and Sojourner Truth.

Referring back to Anthony and Sophia Gay, their first child together was William Anthony Gay (dob 1879) who died of a cerebral hemorrhage in Plaquemine, Louisiana on September 30, 1946. William was married, however the name of his wife is unknown. He is known to have one son, Jacob Gay (dob 1903). A 1910 census shows Jacob was living in Natchez, Mississippi with Lee and Harriet Murray. The relationship to "head of household" is shown as nephew. Harriet is most likely the sister to Jacob's mother. The highest grade completed by William was third grade. His last known occupation was a porter. He worked for Southern Pacific Railroad. The 1940 census lists William Anthony Gay hospitalized at Southern Pacific Sanitarium in Tucson, Arizona. His son Jacob, through oral interviews reportedly as an adult moved to Louisville, Kentucky, where he worked as a dentist. A Kentucky Death Index shows Dr. Jacob A. Gay death date was May 21, 1975.

The second born was Annie Gay Taylor (dob 1881). She was married to Isreal Taylor (dob 1881). Annie, a native of Mississippi and Isreal, a native of Louisiana, it is unclear as to how they met, fell in love and got married. What is interesting about this couple is that she is my great great aunt on my mother's side of the family and Isreal my great great uncle on my father's side. Annie and Isreal never had children.

Their third child was Edward James Gay (dob 1884). A 1910 census shows he is married to Laura Gay. He is known to have one child,

Odessa Gay. Odessa's mother's name is unknown. His draft registration is dated September 12, 1918. A 1920 census shows he is married to Patsy Gay. He was a baker, however his last known occupation may have been a moss picker in the swamps of Louisiana. Oral interview spoke highly of his baking skills. He shared the same "exact" name of a wealthy European who also lived in Plaquemine, Louisiana. On one occasion his social security check in error was mailed to the home of the European Edward James Gay, and he personally delivered the check to him as he wanted to meet the man who had the same name. Edward helped his mother, Sophia take care of his two nieces and nephew following the early death of his sister, Lucile Gay. The 1930 census shows him living in the household of Isreal and Ann Gay Taylor, his sister and brother-in-law. Fortunately, I was able to meet this man during the 1960s. I was about 12 years old. I was told then he was my uncle by my paternal grandmother. I called him Uncle Eddie. At that time he was around 80 years old. My memories of his house being a "cluttered little shack". He used to walk the country gravel roads, waving at us as he passed my grandmother's house. He never talked to us children about my maternal side of the family. He passed away in 1965.

Their fourth child was Clara Gay Scott (dob 1885) who was married to Walter Scott (dob 1892). Walter was also a native of Mississippi. Walter and Clara had one child, Lucille. Clara and Walter moved to Plaquemine around 1920. Clara loved her family. She named her one and only child after her deceased sister, Lucile Gay. On or about this same period, she took into her home her niece, Alma who was 15 years old (the daughter of her deceased sister). Around 1935, Clara sent for her mother and great niece, who lived in Woodville, Mississippi to come to Plaquemine, Louisiana and live with her and her family. Clara also took into her home, her older sister, Annie Gay Taylor, a widower who was gravely ill. Upon the death of her daughter, who passed away at a young age, Clara took care and became guardians to her grandchildren, Gwendolyn who was 6, Clara Ann 4, Clarence, Jr. 3 and Lucille age 2. The baby, Henrietta who was less than a month old was sent to live with her father's side of the family. Her husband, Walter died June 1, 1937 and she died in 1968.

Lucille Gay (dob 1886) was the baby. She never married. Lucille had three children, Alma Swaine, Helen Weathers and Clyde Weathers (aka Clyde Gay). Before her death, Lucille and her three children lived with her mother, Sophia. Lucille's last known occupation was washerwoman. Lucille died about 1912. Despite my efforts to get a copy of her death certificate from Mississippi, it was not available. Alma's father, according to census records may have been Robert Swaine (dob 1881). Alma was darker than her siblings, Helen and Clyde. Helen and Clyde's father, according to census records was James Weathers (dob 1889). The 1990 census shows James Weathers grandfather was Joe Netterville. The 1880 census shows Joe Netterville's race as "mulatto". A mulatto is a term used to refer to a person who is born from one white parent and one black person, or more broadly, a person of mixed black and white ancestry. The term is now considered archaic because of its association with slavery, colonial and social oppression; accepted modern terms include "mixed" and "biracial". Joe Netterville may have been, according to official documents, the son of Jesse Netterville and Nancy Gower Jones. Joe Netterville's daughter, Eliza Netterville is believed to be the mother of James Weathers. Eliza was born about 1868. Sophia Gay's sister, Burnetta was also a Netterville and the 1880 census lists her race as mulatto. In addition, Burnetta's death certificate shows her father was named, Jesse Netterville (dob 1842).

Helen and Clyde were light skinned children. A photo of them at ages 5 and 7 years old is available in this section. Clyde had "straight" hair which was another characteristic of a person of mixed race. Helen's nickname was 'red" referring to her skin color. Helen was my grandmother. The family never spoke of the children's fathers. Upon reaching adulthood, Helen left Woodville and moved to New Orleans. In New Orleans, she found employment as a cook, working in the home of a private family. Helen became pregnant at the age of 22. On June 28, 1929, Helen Weathers and Henry Peterson had a beautiful baby girl. She was named Morell Delores Peterson (my mother). Helen, not married and with unstable living arrangements Morell was sent to Woodville, Mississippi at 3 days old to live with her great grandmother, Sophia who was about 67 years old. I was told that Morell was delivered at a house by a mid-wife and that is the reason there is no birth certificate on file. In my ancestry search, I was able to obtain an application for a social security card she requested while living in Indianapolis, Indiana. Edward James Gay, helped his mother with providing care for Morell. Morell was Helen's only child and needlessly to say they never bonded together or had a mother-daughter relationship. In 1966, in poor health, Helen moved to Los Angeles, California to live with her daughter and son-in-law. Helen died February 20, 1975 and is buried at Greenleaf Cemetery in Compton, California. Morell's father, Henry Peterson was born about 1904 in Mississippi. A 1920 census shows Henry Peterson, 15 years old and his mother Liza Peterson, 55 years old living in West Point, Mississippi, as a boarder. Other household members were the McCoach family. Morell knew her father but never developed a meaningful relationship with him. The 1940 census shows Henry Peterson, at 36 years old was living in New Orleans, and married. His wife was named Bernise Peterson. She was 34 years old. Also in the home was Henry's stepson, Charles Adams born about 1926 and his brothers-in-laws.

The 1940 census shows Sophia Gay was 77 years old and Morell, 9 years. Other household members were Clara Gay Scott, and her daughter, son-in-law and granddaughter, Lucille. They were living in Plaquemine, Louisiana. Sophia's other adult children William, Edward and Annie were also now living in Plaquemine. Morell met the Taylor family while visiting her aunt, Annie Gay Taylor. Morell frequently visited the home of Joseph and Hattie Beatrice Taylor, who would eventually become her in-laws (my grandparents). Their son, Burchmon (my father)had enlisted in the United States Army. Hattie was unable to read and write and would get Morell to write letters for her to Burchmon. Soon a relationship developed between Burchmon and Morell who was discharged from the Army in 1946. At the age of 16 years, Morell and Burchmon were married on January 10, 1946. Sophia seeing that her "baby" would be taken care of died peacefully on February 16, 1947. Sophia died of a cerebral hemorrhage due to senility. Although Sophia Gay's death certificate age was listed as 75 years old, Sophia was at least 84 years old.

In 1946, Morell and Burchmon called Plaquemine, Louisiana. In 1947, they moved to Indianapolis, Indiana and stayed until 1949 when they returned to Plaquemine, Louisiana. My older sister, Barbara Jean was born in 1948 during their stay in Indianapolis. I was born in 1949 when they returned to Plaquemine. In 1951, they moved to New Orleans and my younger sister, Brenda Joyce was born in 1952, in New Orleans. In 1954, at 25 years old Morell was employed at Wise Cafeteria, as a cook. Herbert Wise started the cafeteria in 1933. In 1950, his son Milton Wise bought the cafeteria from his father.

Some of the cafeteria's favorites were fried chicken, red beans, mashed potatoes, green beans, bread pudding and chocolate cake. Burchmon was employed at Public Grain Elevator. The term "grain elevator" is used to refer to a storage facility where grain is moved into rail cars or ships for transport. Burchmon's job was handling of bulky bins and loading them on barges (ships). Like any couple, Morell and Burchmon had problems which eventually caused them to separate after years of marriage. In 1960, the couple separated. Burchmon moved to Los Angeles, California. Morell remained in New Orleans with the three children. In 1965, Morell moved to California with the three children to live with Burchmon. In 1970, Burchmon and Morell separated again and remained living apart. However, although living separate lives they were always there for one another in times of need.

GENERATION I	II	III	IV
DESCENDANTS OF			
WILLIAM VEAL OF TENNESSEE	Henry 1817 -	Rufus 1859-	
	William 1820-	Marcus 1862-	
	Robert 1826-	Silas 1866-	
William Veal 1802-1885	**Mary (Gay) 1836-**	Melia 1852-	
& Mary 1812-1890	Duncan 1838-	Ollie 1855-	
of Maryland	Kitty 1840-	Richmond 1864-	
	Noland 1848-	Jim 1870-	
	Charlotte 1851-	Tamar 1872-	
	Preston 1853-	Emily 1874-	
	Florence 1854-	Lydia 1884-	
	Alvira 1855-	Willie 1884-	
		Edward 1882-	
		Ida 1887-	
		Ella 1889-	
		Mamie 1898-	
		Mary 1855-1925	Frank 1875-
		Anthony Gay	Walter 1877-
		1857-1935	
			Peter 1879-
			Nolan 1885-
			Mary 1888-
			Millie 1889-
			William 1894-
			Mattie 1896-
			William 1878-1946
			Annie 1881-1954
			Edward James
			1884-1966
			Clara 1885-1968
			Lucille 1886-1911

Death certificate of Peter Veal, he is believed to be the grandson of my great great great great grandfather, William Veal who was born in 1802. The Veals appeared to hold such jobs as carriagemen, carpenters, cooks and other domestic positions other than fieldwork.

Land record document showing 81 acres homesteaded to Robert Veal signed by President Theodore Roosevelt dated February 13, 1905.

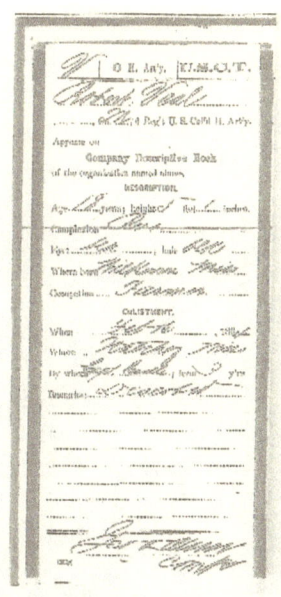

My ancestor, Robert Veal, at age 18 years old served
in the United States Colored Troops (USCT).

Anthony Gay, my great great grandfather (185-1935).

Sophie Taylor Gay, my great great grandmother (1862-1947).

William Gay (1879-1946) PICTURE NOT SHOWN

**William Gay, my great great uncle (1879-
1946) PICTURE NOT SHOWN.**

Annie Gay Taylor, my great great aunt (1881—1954).

Edward James Gay, my great gtreat uncle (1884-1966).

Clara Gay Scott, my great great aunt (1885-1968).

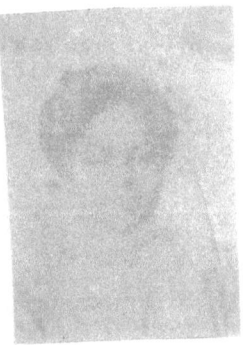

Lucille Gay, my great grandmother (1886-1911).

THE TAYLORS

According to the 1880 census, my Taylor ancestor, Isreal Taylor was born about 1827 and Effie Taylor, born about 1829 in North Carolina. Isreal's siblings were Armstead Taylor (dob 1819) and Dennis Taylor (dob 1830). He also had a sister-in-law, Adeline Taylor (dob 1820). Based on the birth of Isreal's son, William Taylor (dob 1857) in Louisiana, Isreal most likely migrated to or was sold to another slaveholder between 1845 and 1855

North Carolina, a state that was part of the thirteen colonies, had a port on the Atlantic Coast where Africans from various tribes were shipped to the United States. During this period, tobacco and cotton were being abundantly produced and there was a desire for slave labor. Tobacco stimulated North Carolina farmers to begin growing tobacco as a cash crop in the late 1850s. A North Carolina farmer named Washington Duke turned to the cultivation of tobacco when his cotton failed. Mr. Duke cultivated tobacco until his farming operation was interrupted by the civil war. Washington Duke was born about 1820. He was the son of Taylor Duke. Washington Duke joined the Confederate Army in 1863 or early 1864. Because of a shortage of troops the confederate government enacted laws which forced men up to the age of forty-five to join the service. It is also known that some slaves fought in the Confederate Army.

Union troops sampling of bright leaf tobacco led Washington Duke's decision to market this "golden weed". His vision and others created a market that eventually would transform North Carolina into a world-wide tobacco empire. Duke and his sons began mass production of cigarettes. Many of the profits were used to invest in land and to develop fast-growing southern industries such as electric power and textiles, and humanitarian causes. Trinity College, later to become Duke University, benefitted from the family contributions. As part of my visit to Durham-Raleigh, North Carolina, a state where my ancestors once lived I was able to tour the Washington Duke's restored family home, a factory, a curing barn and a pack house where Washington Duke grew and processed tobacco. I also toured the Tobacco museum which traces tobacco history from Native Americans to the present, included in the tour was the Stagville Plantation. The Bennehan-Cameron families were among those in pre-civil war North Carolina, by 1860 owning almost 30,000 acres and nearly 600 slaves.

I was fortunate to have a tour of the home of James and Nancy Bennett, simple yeoman farmers that served as the site of the surrender negotiations between general Joseph E. Johnston and General William T. Sherman April 17, 18 and 26, 1865. The farm of James and Nancy Bennett was chosen by the Confederate Army because it was the closest and most convenient place for privacy. It was the largest surrender of the American Civil War, officially ending the fighting in Florida, Georgia, South Carolina and North Carolina, totaling 89,270 soldiers, the largest group to surrender during the war. James and Nancy Bennett was a typical family living in America at the time of the American Civil War. Average middle class, the Bennetts were considered farmers who owned a small acreage, working the land themselves and providing for themselves through their skills of sewing, making and repairing tools, and other aspects of self-sufficiency. The Bennett family never owned slaves as this was a very expensive business. My tour of North Carolina historical sites along with an abundant amount of research was helpful in getting a clear understanding of what it might have been like living during that period.

It is unknown as to how my ancestors derived the surname of Taylor or even how they migrated from North Carolina to Plaquemine. During my earlier research, I thought it was going to lead me to a connection with President Zachary Taylor. I had found information that President Zachary Taylor had a farm in Baton Rouge, Louisiana, a town nearby Plaquemine, Louisiana where my ancestors lived. In addition, Zachary, Louisiana is about 26 miles from Plaquemine, Louisiana. I also learned that President Zachary Taylor had a son named Richard Taylor and that I had a great great uncle named Richard Taylor (dob 1883). However, I also learned that my paternal great great great grandfather was named "Richard" Martin and that he may have derived the name "Richard" from him, his grandfather. Even with this information I still had a burning desire to further explore how my Taylor ancestors might have received the surname "Taylor". This lead me back to the descendent of President Zachary Taylor. My initial findings began in the early 1800s.

Richard Lee Taylor was born in 1744 and died in 1829. He was born in Orange County, Virginia to Zachary Taylor and Elizabeth Lee. In 1799, he married Sarah Strother. Richard and Sarah had a total of nine children. President Zachary Taylor was the 3rd son, born in 1784. One brother was named Hancock. One of the brothers sold a parcel of land in Tyrell County, North Carolina reportedly to Richard (President Zachary's father) and another brother. Leaving exhausted land in North Carolina, Richard and his family joined the westward movement and settled near Louisville, Kentucky (see map 1-2). He owned around 10,000 acres throughout Kentucky and had 26 slaves (could my great great great grandfather Isreal Taylor been one of those slaves which would account for the migration of my Taylor ancestry from North Carolina to Kentucky to Louisiana) to cultivate the land. In 1800, Richard Lee Taylor was a very prominent and wealthy planter and landowner. Richard Lee Taylor was the father of the 12th President of the United States.

President Zachary Taylor was born in Barbourville, Virginia. He was the 3rd of 5 surviving sons in his family (a son died in infancy) and had three younger sisters. In 1810, President Zachary Taylor married Margaret Smith. They had a total of six children. In the late 1820s the family moved to a plantation near Baton rouge, Louisiana. He owned a second plantation in Mississippi, called Cypress Grove. President Zachary Taylor was a career military officer and commanded several forts, where his family could live with him. He also was a wealthy and prominent landowner and planter. In 1847, President Taylor OWNED more than 300 slaves. Supposedly he never sold a slave. Due to President Zachary Taylor's military duties he was seldom at home. The plantations were run by overseers. He kept close watch on the activities of his plantations. Reportedly, his slaves, or "servants" as he referred to them were treated well. I found it very interesting when I saw an 1880 census my great great great aunt Deline Taylor (dob 1820) under "occupation" showed "servant". Besides cotton crops, President Zachary Taylor raised other things such as sheep, cattle, hogs, tobacco, corn, etc. He also put the slaves to work logging. This effort was so successful that the plantation invested in its own sawmill. In my research of my Taylor ancestors, I found that they had a work history of working in the swamps of Louisiana, cutting down large cypress trees, loading them up and transporting them to a sawmill, for processing. My Taylor ancestors appeared to be tall, large and strong in stature, very capable of being what is sometimes referred to as lumberjacks. However back then they were called "swampers". President Zachary Taylor, out of six children, he had one son, Richard Taylor, named for his grandfather.

Richard Taylor, the son of President Zachary Taylor was born in 1826. In 1851 he married Marie Myrthe Bringier of Louisiana. They had 5 children, 3 girls and 2 boys. Both sons died of scarlet fever during the civil war. Richard Taylor was a prominent landowner, planter, politician and one of the confederacy's most effective generals. With Cypress Grove Plantation in Mississippi and Fashion Plantation in Louisiana, he was one of the richest men in the state. Richard Taylor inherited both plantations from his father, President Zachary Taylor when he died in 1850. In 1853, Frederick Lee Olmstead, a New York Times reporter, published several articles on the savagery of the institution of slavery in the South. In my research on this reporter I was able to obtain one such article of an incident he witnessed and reported in the New York Daily Times currently known as the New York Times, as he accompanied an overseer on a tour of a large plantation in Mississippi. The article is entitled "Life on a Southern Plantation, 1854 – A glimpse of the south before the civil war. He discussed in this article how he happened to see the severest corporal punishment of a young Negro woman he ever saw. Apparently, she was caught with a bunch of keys on her person and the overseer without allowing the young woman to explain or verify her story she was told by the overseer to pull up her clothes, lie down and was beaten with a rawhide type of belt and given 30 to 40 lashes across her naked body, with as much strength as he could. This is just an example and reminder of the horrific life those that were enslaved had to endure. Mr. Olmstead wrote a positive report on Richard Taylor stating that under the care of Richard Taylor, his "servants" appeared to be well-cared. The "servants" ate from the same stores and gardens as the Taylor Family. A physician was held on retainer to provide them medical care. The slaves were given Sundays off from their labor and received time off for holidays and special events, such as funerals. Richard Taylor died in 1879. He is buried in Metarie, Louisiana.

Richard Taylor's Fashion Plantation was located in Hahnville, Louisiana. When in operation, it had over 200 slaves. With the civil war, the plantation was completely demolished by federal troops. To date, the grounds that once held this plantation is a subdivision of homes and referred to as Fashion Plantation Estates. In the Great Flood of 1927 the Mississippi river spread out for 100 miles south of Memphis and over 1,000 people in Mississippi lost their lives. The Cypress Grove Plantation caved in and fell into the Mississippi River. The "Black" Taylor and the "European" Taylor family appear to have a connection to both North Carolina and Virginia. Did my Taylor ancestors once lived on the "European" Taylor plantation? Did my ancestors take on the "Taylor" surname following their freedom? An official document show my great great great grandfather, Isreal Taylor was born in North Carolina in 1827, President Zachary Taylor's father, Richard Taylor has a history in North Carolina; An official document shows Isreal's mother's birthplace in Virginia – President Zachary Taylor's father, Richard Taylor was born in Orange County, Virginia and President Zachary Taylor was born in Barbourville, Virginia.

Isreal had two known sons, William (dob 1857) and Charles (dob 1862). Official documents show that he married Affay in 1864. William married Dora Martin about 1876. They had six children – Elvira (dob 1878); William (dob 1879) – my great great grandfather; Dennis (dob 1882); Richard (dob 1883) and Andrew (dob 1885). William appears on the 1880 census at the age 0f 28 years old, as head of household. On the 1900 census, Dora appears as head of household with five children – Willie, Dennis, Isreal, Richard and Andrew. Her half-brother Hollison (Harris), 22 years old was also a member of the household. The Civil War Pension Index show a William Taylor with Dora Taylor as widower, the date of death 08/03/1915. William and Dora may have been married between 1880 and 1915, but separated. During these times you would not think of such a thing, at least I didn't, but also found that there were marital problems with my maternal great great great grandparents, Anthony and Sophia Gay who also separated during this same period.

William and Dora's first child, Elvira (dob 1878) was probably named for William's mother "Ellie". She married to Arthur Blackwell on August 25, 1898. Elvira and Arthur had one child, a daughter named Bertha (dob February 1896). Elvira's brothers would stay with her and her family. The brothers worked as swampers and earned money to help their mother with living expenses. During this period, one of the most popular jobs for Blacks with very little education was working in the swamps of Louisiana, cutting down trees, loading the trees on waiting trucks that was used to make lumber. The workers sometimes had to leave home for months to do this type of work. Gone for months, they would often send their earnings home by other swampers. The 1910 census shows that Elvira is a widower and living in New Orleans, other members of the household is her 14 year old daughter, Bertha and her mother, Dora Taylor. Elvira is 32 years old and working as a laundress for a private family. A laundress during this period is defined as one who washed and iron clothes for a private family. Bertha died August 30, 1927, tuberculosis of the lungs.

William Joseph Taylor aka Willie Taylor (dob 1879) was the second born of William and Dora. William was a tall, slender and good looking man. He married Pinky Chatman, the daughter of Arthur and Elsie Chatman. Arthur (dob 1869) was born in Virginia. His father was William (dob 1832) and Lucy (dob 1834) Chatman both born in Virginia. Willie and Pinky was married on May 15, 1902. Pinky had three siblings – Mary (dob 1888); King (dob 1890); and Daisey (1892). Pinky was born in 1885 and died July 30, 1920 with fibroid of the uterus. Willie and Pinky had six children. Herbert Isreal (dob 1903 and died in 1958). Beulah was the second born (dob 1904 and she died in 1989). Joseph Willie, my grandfather was the third born (dob 1906 and he died in 1978). Leola (dob 1909) the fourth born and died at the age of five years old. Her cause of death is unknown. Andrew (dob 1911) was the fifth born. Andrew, at six years old died July 29, 1917 of "dropsy". Dropsy is an old term for Edema. Edema is an excessive accumulation of watery fluid in body cavities. Edema could result from multiple causes including allergy, protein deficiency and congestive heart failure. Grace Elizabeth (dob 1912 and died in 1946) was the sixth born. She never married. She had one son, Herbert Isreal Taylor (dob June 24, 1934 and died June2, 2008). Willie (William) must have been going through some difficult times during the periods of 1917 and 1920. His wife Pinky was ill and died during this time. His World War I Draft record dated September 12, 1918 show that he was employed as a farm laborer for farm Bureau Fertilizer Company. William also once was lived on the St. Louis Plantation and was employed by Edward J. Gay Printing and Manufacturing Company in Plaquemine, Louisiana. I developed an interest in this company because my maternal great great uncle was named Edward J. Gay (see Veal/Gay section for more information).

The European Edward James Gay (Willie's employer was born about February 3, 1816 and died May 30, 1889. He was a financier and a member of the United States Congress. An 1870 census shows that an Edward J. Gay. His "occupation" is merchant and farmer. His "estate value" is $700,000 and his "personal estate" valued at $60,000. He married Lavenia Hynes in 1840. Mr. Gay was born in Liberty, Bedford County, Virginia, which is where an 1870 census REPORTS that my great great uncle Edward James Gay's grandmother, Nancy Jones was born. Is there a connection between the European Gay and the Black Gay family? The European Edward James Gay moved from Virginia to Illinois around 1820 and later the family migrated to St. Louis, Missouri and finally to Louisiana. In 1857, Mr. Gay built The St. Louis Plantation, naming it for the city of St. Louis. Today, the property is listed on the National Register of Historic places. It is reported that the European Gay is of English and French descent, and a branch of the family descended from Pochantas.

Isreal is the third born of William and Dora. Isreal, born in 1881 and the cause of his death was accidental. An oral interview states that he was tying a horse to a cart, the horse bucked and caused the cart to turn over and fall on him. He died of a broken neck. He was married to my great great aunt, Annie Gay. Dennis was the fourth born and very little is known about him. An oral interview reports that his death was also caused by an accident, a tree fell on him. Like his brothers he also worked in the swamps of Louisiana, cutting down trees and loading them on trucks to be processed for lumber.

Richard (dob 1883) was the fifth child of William and Dora. He was married to Ellanora (Elenoria, Norah and Elenora) Irvin. Ellanora was a twin. Her twin was named Delia. Richard and Ellanora had one child, a daughter named Veola Taylor Chillis. I found this information during my search in a Land Purchase Agreement document. His World War I Draft Registration Card dated June 5, 1917 shows that he was a widower, with one child and his employer as F. B. William Cypress Company (Bell River Camp Camp) Morgan City, Louisiana. I wanted to know more about this company, especially since in my search I found that my ancestors worked as "swampers", cutting down trees and loading them on trucks. My uncle Dennis, possibly cause of death behind such dangerous work. The F. B. William Cypress Company became one of the largest lumber companies in the United

States. Francis Bennett Williams (known as Frank B. Williams) was also known as The Cypress King. He was an ingenious and ambitious person. He acquired thousands of acres of cypress bearing swampland in Louisiana and began a timber harvesting and milling operation. Mr. Williams promoted the selling of cypress national and international markets. Frank B. Williams imagination and financial genius gave employment to thousands of workers and sped the development of southern Louisiana as a pioneer in the cypress lumber industry.

Andrew (dob 1885) was the sixth son of William and Dora, and apparently the most adventurous. The 1930 census lists Andrew's home in Indianapolis, Indiana. Andrew was married to Ethel, a native of Indiana. Looking for work, his brother Willie later joined him in Indianapolis, also my parents, Burchmon and Morell. In 1948, my oldest sister Barbara Jean was born in Indianapolis. As part of my journey in a quest to "walk in the footsteps" of my descendent Indianapolis, Indiana was included on the lists of places for me to visit. My visit to Indianapolis was very enlightening. It started out with me just wanting to see the area my descendent once lived, however once there I could see why Andrew was prompted to leave the small town of Plaquemine and migrate to the city of Indianapolis. By the 1890's, in Indianapolis, African Americans had established a vibrant social, commercial and economic community. Black entertainers, entrepreneurs, politicians and working people developed the community into a thriving widely known neighborhood of theaters, jazz clubs, stores, offices and residences. In 1910, Madame C. J. Walker (wife of Charles J. Walker) started a legacy in Indianapolis. The daughter of ex-slaves, she was born Sarah Breedlove in 1867 in Delta, Louisiana. In 1910, Many Blacks moved north and west to escape the massive backlash of racism that followed Reconstruction. Madame C. J. Walker was a self-made millionaire. She literally turned a $1.50 investment into the nation's largest black hair care company. Besides the many Europeans (Edward J. Gay, Taylor Duke, Francis B. Williams) that history and even this book speak of in regards to contributions that have made this such a great nations, very little is passed down as to the accomplishments of Blacks. During my visit in Indianapolis, I visited the home site of President Benjamin Harrison (1889-1893) our 23rd president. He was born in Ohio in 1833 and moved to Indianapolis in 1854. He died in 1901. I was interested in this particular president because he was born, lived and served as president of the United States during the period that I was most interested in researching my ancestry. Research on this president provided me with key developments and important events that helped shaped our nation's history. His grandfather, President William Henry Harrison (dob 1773-1841) was our 9th president (1841). Yes the date is correct. President William Henry Harrison spent only 31 days in office. He is the president most remembered for the brevity of his term in office. He died a month after his inauguration. During President Benjamin Harrison term as president, six states were admitted to the union – North Dakota, South Dakota, Montana, Idaho, Washington and Wyoming. In 1890, The House of Representatives passed the Force Bill to protect Black voters in the South, however the Senate refused to pass it. Does that sound familiar with what is happening with current Democrat and Republican politicians and our current President Barack Obama? The Dependent Pension Act was passed to give money to veterans injured in war. The Sherman Antitrust Act prevented big businesses from creating trusts and the McKinley Tariff was enacted to make Americans buy more products made in the United States.

Going back to the second generation, Willie and Pinky's first born was Herbert (dob 1902. Herbert was married to Virgie Taylor. Herbert and Virgie had two known children, Andrew Lee and Grace Elizabeth. They were named for Herbert' youngest brother, and sister. During my research, one thing that that stood out with my Taylor ancestors is the naming of generation after generation for mothers, fathers, brothers, sisters and uncles. Herbert Isreal Taylor died March 1, 1958.

Beulah was the second born (dob 1904) to Willie and Pinky. She was married to Felton Brown. She was 18 years old when she left home and married Felton. The 1930 census shows her home in New Orleans. She has also lived in Chicago, Illinois; Indianapolis, Indiana and before her death, she moved to Los Angeles, California. Felton died about 1960 and Beulah never remarried. Her occupation was housework for a private family. In 980, her move to Los Angeles allowed her to have more family contact with her nephews and niece who had already moved to Los Angeles – Burchmon Joseph, Sylvester Willie, Andrew Lee and Grace Elizabeth. As children, we all thought Aunt Beulah looked and acted mean, like her brother, my grandfather, Joseph Willie (J.W.) but later decided that it was just being a "Taylor". Beulah died in 1989 in Los Angeles, California and is buried in the Inglewood Cemetery.

Joseph Willie (J.W.) was the third born (dob 1906) to Willie and Pinky. Also at 18 years old like his older sister Beulah, he married Hattie Beatrice Asberry, who was then 22 years old. Their first son was Burchmon, my father. Joseph Willie and Hattie Beatrice married in 1924. Their second child, Sylvester Willie was born in 1932.As a young girl I always saw J. W. and Hattie as an odd couple. He was very tall, and mean. J. W. was a good provider despite his frequent absences. With the passing away of most of the Taylor line, J. W. with his family lived on the property originally purchased by his grandparents, William and Dora Taylor. To ensure that the property ownership would remain with his family he bought out any known heirs or persons of interest in the land. In 1930, the property according to an official document was valued at $800. Upon the death of J. W. and Burchmon, the property was sold September 4, 1996 in the amount of $53,000. The property was sold to Little Rock Baptist Church, where J. W. and Hattie Beatrice were once members. Joseph Willie (J.W.) loved his family. He died in 1978.

Burchmon (dob 1922) was married to Morell Peterson. He served in World War II. Burchmon enlisted in the army July 25, 1942, at a time the United States was deeply in war with Germany. This war lasted from 1939-1945. Burchmon and Morell had three children. Barbara Jean (dob 1948) ; Patricia Ann (dob 1949) and Brenda Joyce (dob 1952). Burchmon did not complete high school. He was last employed by the United States Veterans Administration as a custodian for eighteen years. He died of cancer, March 1983. Sylvester Willie (dob 1932), Burchmon's only brother upon reaching eighteen, enlisted in the United States Navy around 1950. The Korean War lasted from June 25, 1950 – July 27, 1953. The Korean War was conflict between communist and non-communist forces in Korea. After serving his time in the navy, he married Cora Brown. They had one son, Carl Wayne. Sylvester and his new family moved to Los Angeles, California around 1954. Prior to 1968, Sylvester and Cora were divorced and Sylvester married Maggie Holmes. Sylvester and Maggie had three children Sharon Lynn; Jacqueline Beatrice and Brian Joseph. Sylvester was employed by Los Angeles City Department of Water and Power for at least twenty years. Sylvester was very passionate about his love for his mother and brother. It was just the opposite with his father. I always attributed that this attitude because he did not like the way his mother was treated by his father, which included having children outside the marriage and his father's frequent absences away from the family. Sylvester died of cancer November 18, 2002.

Barbara Jean (dob 1948) was the first born of Burchmon and Morell. She was married to Clifford Risin and following a divorce married Arthur Ivory. Barbara and Clifford had one daughter, Demetria Risin (dob 1967). Barbara had a second child, Bridgette Hardy (dob 1979). Bridgette's father is Ulysses Hardy. Barbara Jean died of cancer on April 14, 1989. Patricia Ann was the second born (dob 1949) to Burchmon and Morell. Her first born is Tracie Marie Denise Hawkins Gaines (dob 1968). Tracie's father is Billy Ray Hawkins. In 1973, Patricia married William "Billy" Mopkins. Patricia and William have three children – William Jr. (dob 1973); Dawn Millette (dob 1978) and Taylor Ashley (dob 1983). William, Jr was born with multiple medical problems and died January 5, 2011. The cause of death was pneumonia. Brenda Joyce the third born (dob 1952) had three children – Sharnee (dob 1969) Damien (dob 1979) and Brandon (dob 1983).

GENERATION I	II	III	IV
DESCEBDANTS OF			
Isreal Taylor of North Carolina			
Isreal 1827	William 1857-1915	Elvira 1878-	Herbert Isreal 1903-56
& Affay 1829-		William 1879-	Beulah 1904-1989
		Isreal 1881-1945	Joseph Willie 1906-78
		Dennis 1882-1922	Leola 1909-1915
		Richard 1883-	Andrew 1911-1917
		Andrew1885-	Grace Elizabeth 1912-

V	VI	VII
Andrew Lee 1935-	Barbara Jean 1948-1989	Demetria 1967-
Grace Elizabeth 1937-2009	Patricia Ann 1949-	Bridgette 1979-
Burchmon Joseph 1922-1983	Brenda Joyce 1952-	Tracie 1968-
Sylvester Willie 1932-2002	William, Jr. 1973-2011	
Herbert Isreal 1934-2008	Sharon 1963-	Dawn 1978-
	Carl Wayne 1955-	Taylor 1983-
	- Jacqueline 1965-2004	
		Sharnee 1971
	Brian 1968-	Damien 1976-
		Brandon 1984-
	Grace Elizabeth 1959-?	
	Michael 1961-	

William Taylor, my great great grandfather (1879-).

Elvira Taylor Blackwell, my great great aunt (1878 -).

Isreal Taylor, my great great Uncle (1881-1945) and his wife Annie Gay Taylor.

The Taylors home. This property was purchased by
William Taylor prior to 1930, During that time it was
valued at $800. In 1996 it sold for $53000.

A picture of a bald cypress tree in a Louisiana swamp. The
trees were cut down by laborers and used as timber. My
Taylor ancestors job occupations were called Swampers.

My great aunts, Beulah Taylor Brown and
Grace Elizabeth Taylor around 1920's.

My great uncle, Herbert Israel Taylor (1903-1956)

My father, Burchmon Joseph Taylor (1922-1983). He served
in the United States Army during World War II.

THE MARTINS

Isaac Martin (dob 1812) was born in Maryland. He was married to Patsey Martin (dob 1811). Patsey was born in Petersburg (Independent City) Virginia. Petersburg, Virginia was founded December 17, 1782. It was an independent in Virginia located on the Appomattox River and twenty-three miles from Richmond, Virginia. The city location was used as a transportation hub to create wealth for Virginia. Petersburg had one of the oldest settlements in the state at Pocahontas Island. Following the Revolutionary War, inspired by the Revolution's principles of equality, many Virginia slaveholders manumitted their slaves. THIS probably accounts for my great great great grandmother, Patsey Martin status on the 1860 census as a "Free Inhabitant". The number of free blacks in Virginia rose between 1782 and 1810. A "free Black" was the term used prior to the abolition of slavery in the United States. The "free Black" drew from multiple sources: 1) children born of free colored persons 2) mulatto children born of free colored mothers 3) mulatto children born of white servants or free women 4) children of free Blacks and Indian parentage 5) manumitted slaves (freed by owner and 6) slaves who escaped. Slaveholders manumitted slaves for various reasons. An owner died and the heir did not want slaves, freed as a reward for his or her good service, the slave was able to pay for his freedom, or promise of freedom for serving in the army. In my research, Patsey Martin is my only known ancestor to have the status of a "free person" prior to 1865.

The 1860 census shows my great great great grandmother, Patsey had migrated to Plaquemine, Louisiana. It is not known as to what, how or who initiated the move. It just makes one wonder what prompts a person of "free' status living in an independent city, move to a southern state where the enslaved received such horrific treatment. The 1860 census showed Patsey household members included her husband Isaac and their three grandchildren Cornelius (dob 1852); Richard (dob 1857) and William (dob 1859). Isaac and Patsey had four known sons – Richard (dob 1835) my great

great grandfather; Albert (dob 1837); George (dob 1840) and Isaac Jr. (dob 1844). Isaac Martin, Sr. had one known brother, William Martin (dob 1810). Isaac Martin, Sr. died April 21, 1875. Patsey's date of death is not known.

My great great grandfather, Richard Martin was born in Louisiana. He was married to Charlotte Watkins (dob 1840). Richard and Charlotte had five known children – Cornelius (dob 1852); William (dob 1859); Medora (dob 1860) my great great grandmother; Julia (dob 1862) and Richard (dob 1864). Richard's second wife was Mary Harris. Richard had another known six children with Mary – Sirrus (dob 1866); Harris (dob 1873); Rachael (dob 1874); Mandy (dob 1876); Frances (dob 1877) and Westley (dob 1878). An 1850 census shows Richard's (who was around fifteen years old) home at Christ Church in Charleston, South Carolina. He was listed with several others in this Episcopalian Group. Being enslaved, he was most likely taken to South Carolina for free labor to build this church. History tells us that the enslaved was used in many areas, including carpentry. My research found that there was a groundbreaking in 1852 for Christ Church Episcopalian in Greenville, South Carolina. The church was built with stone and stucco trim and completed in 1854. The church is now listed on the National Register of Historic Places. Charleston (Charles Town), South Carolina was home to a mixture of ethnic and religious groups. French, Scottish, Irish and Germans migrated to the developing town, representing numerous Protestant denominations, as well as Roman Catholicism, Judaism and Jews.

Albert was the second born to Isaac and Patsey. He was married to Elsy Martin and they had six known children – Isaac (dob 1860); Kitto (dob 1862) Adam (dob 1864); William (dob 1865); Nancy (1867); and Albert, Jr. (dob 1869). George was the third son of Isaac and Patsey. He was born about 1840 and died March 6, 1925. He was married to Clara Martin. Albert and Clara had four known children –Estelle (dob 1860); Henry (dob 1862); Wade (dob 1886 and died September 27, 1923) and Sarah (dob 1869). Isaac, Jr. was the fourth son. He was born in 1844 and died in 1950. Isaac was married to Josephine (dob 1849) Martin and they had three known children – Isaac, Jr. (dob 1883); Samuel (dob 1886) and Arthur (dob 1889). The 1870 census listed the Martin Family. It included Isaac, Patsey, their four sons and the names of their sons' families.

Very little is known about this side of my family but I felt the necessity to include, as a tree has many "branches". My great great great grandmother (Dora) was a "MARTIN" who happened to marry a "TAYLOR".

GENERATION I	II	III	IV
DESCENDANTS			
OF Isaac Martin			
(of Maryland)			
		Cornelius 1857-	Elvira 1878-
	Richard 1835-	William 1858	William 1879-1950
	& Charlotte	Medora 1868-	Isreal 1881-1945
	& Mary	Julia 1862-	Dennis 1882-?
		Richard 1864-	Richard 1883-1920
		Sirrus 1866-	Andrew 1885- ?
	Albert 1837-	Harris 1873-	
	& Elsy	Rachel 1874	
		Mandy 1876	
Isaac 1812-1875	George 1840- 1925	Isaac 1860-	
Martin	&Clara	Kitto 1862-	
& Patsey 1815-?	Adam 1864-		
Of Virginia	William 1865-		
		Nancy 1867 –	
		Albert, Jr. 1868-	
	Isaac 1844 -1919	Estelle 1860-	
	&	Henry 1862-	
	Josephine	Wade 1866-	
		Sarah 1868-	
		Isaac 1883-	
		Samuel 1886-	
		Arthur 1889-	
William 1810-?			
Martin			

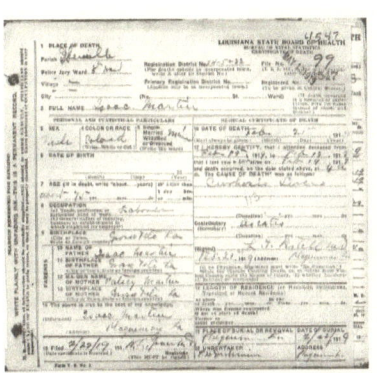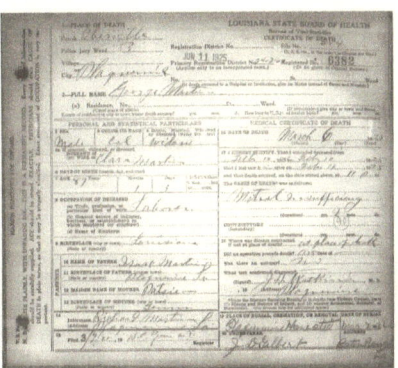

Death certificates of my great great uncles born respectively 1838 and 1844. Before their death both knew what it was like to live as a slave. Their parents were probably direct descendents from Africa.

THE ASBERRYS

My great great great grandfather, Isaac Asberry (dob 1820) was born in Virginia. He was married to Julia Asberry (dob 1820) who was also born in Virginia. Isaac and Julia are known to have three sons – my great great grandfather William Asberry (dob 1841); later, the name "William Asberry" will be carried over at least five future generations; Isaac (dob 1844) the second son and Louis George (dob 1845) the third son. At some point, Isaac and Julia left Virginia and migrated to Mississippi.

Isaac and Julia's first son, my great great grandfather, William Asberry (dob 1841) was born in Mississippi. He was married to Nancy Asberry (dob 1822). Nancy was born in Virginia. Nancy probably migrated to Mississippi along with William's parents, Isaac and Julia, as they were around the same age. Her mother and father were most likely Africans that were taken from their homeland and brought to the United States. An 1870 census shows William and Nancy living in Warren, Mississippi. Records show that William had two sons with his second wife, Lizzie White, William Asberry, Jr. (dob 1860) and George (dob 1879).

Isaac, Jr. was the second son of Isaac Sr. and Julia Asberry. He was married to Mary Asberry. They had four known children – Amos (dob 1881); Isaac "Ike" (dob 1886);Aaron (dob 1888) and Levia (dob 1891). Isaac, Jr. died May 16, 1950. Amos Asberry is listed as the informant on his death certificate. Isaac Asberry Jr. last place of residence is East Baton Rouge, Louisiana.

Louis George was the third son of Isaac, Sr. and Julia Asberry. It is unknown if he was married or had children. His World War I Draft Registration is dated May 16, 1917. This document describes Louis George as "short", which is a known characteristic for the Asberrys. He died May 16, 1918, according to the Louisiana Statewide Death Index.

My great grandfather, William Asberry, Jr. (dob 1860) was married to Katie Bray/Katie Lewis. His World War I Draft Registration dated September 12, 1918 shows his occupation as a field laborer and his employer was A. Wilbert & Sons. In my research, I found that an Antonius Wilbert, a German settled in Plaquemine in the 1830s. Antonius Wilbert, one of many Europeans who came to the new nation where rewarded with land and opportunity. Antonius Wilbert & Son purchased The Myrtle Grove Plantation in 1905. The Myrtle Grove Plantation was located five miles from Plaquemine, Louisiana. It was a sugar plantation. It was in operation from the late 1890s until December 26, 1976, when it closed. William and Katie had four known children – Doreatha (dob 1900); Hattie Beatrice (dob 1902) my grandmother; William III (dob 1907); and Katie (dob 1910). His second wife was Celia Washington. He married her on May 19, 1913. William and Celia had five known children – Herman (dob 1914); Ruth (dob 1916); Isaac (dob 1917); Thelma (dob 1919) and Douglas (dob 1921). Celia had two known children prior to her marriage to William, Ila (dob 1904) and Gertrude (dob 1906). Celia Washington is the daughter of Isaac and Clarinda Washington. Isaac (dob 1845) was born in Charleston, South Carolina. Celia Asberry died August 21, 1961.

George (dob 1879) was the second son of William, Sr. and Lizzie Asberry. He was married to Appolia, aka Ophelia Spriggs. They were married on February 27, 1899. George and Ophelia had nine known children – Clarence (dob 1901); Wilma (dob 1903); Leona (dob 1904); George, Jr. (1907); Theola (dob 1908); Edna (dob 1913); Roland (dob 1914); Burchmon (dob 1915); and Velma (dob 1917). My father, Burchmon Joseph Taylor most likely derived the name Burchmon from Burchmon Asberry, who is the first cousin of his mother, Hattie Beatrice Asberry Taylor.

My great grandfather, William Asberry, Jr. first born was Doretha. She never married and had no children. In 1955, Aunt Doe had a tragic accident that nearly cost her life. She lived alone in a trailer. Propane gas was often used for heating. One day, the propane gas tank exploded and caused a huge fire inside the trailer. Aunt Doe survived, but was scarred for life with facial burns. She saved her life by jumping into the nearby Bayou Gross Tete.

Hattie Beatrice, my grandmother was the second born. Doretha and Hattie had a very close relationship. Hattie had a kind heart and was loved by the community. She was called many names – shorty, fat, Hattie B. and Dewey. She remains my favorite person to this date. William III, was the third born. He married Olevia Washington and had eleven children Clarence (dob 1927); Isaac "Ike" (dob 1929); Learthe (dob 1931); William George "pie", IV (dob 1934); Norman (dob 1936); Lawrence (dob 1939); Earnest (dob 1942); Mary "Elizabeth" (dob 1945): Leonard (dob 1946); Barbara Jean (dob 1949) and Roland (dob 1954). William, III died on May 9, 1955, his son Roland was only one years old. Katie was the fourth child. She married Josh Robertson and had eleven known children having three sets of twins – Herman (dob 1926); Joseph (dob 1929); Charlie (dob 1931); Ream and Rome (twins dob 1935); Floyd (dob 1937); Leola and Leon (twins dob 1939); Shirley (dob 1938) and Lovie and Clarence (dob 1940. Herman, Sr. was the fifth child. He was married to Victoria Hunter. They had one son, Herman "Tony", Jr. and Herman had two other children, Beatrice and another daughter. Herman, Sr. died December 18, 1989. Ruth was the sixth born. She like Doretha, never married but had one son. Ruth died in 1939, three days after giving birth to her son, Joseph. Isaac is the seventh born. He died June 22, 1994. Thelma was the eighth born. She was married to Arthur Doakes and they had three known children – Peter, Celia and Gracie. Thelma died March 1984. Douglas was the ninth born. He was married to Elouise Jones. Douglas had two known sons, Douglas, Jr. and Edward Bruce. Oral interviews reports Douglas, Jr. mother died giving birth to Douglas, Jr. Daisy Brown is the mother of Edward Bruce.

Although my search of the Asberry branch begins in Virginia, then Mississippi and later Louisiana there were earlier descendent from Africa. Besides, the spelling Asberry, it was also spelled Asbury. Hopefully, future generations will use whatever information I have obtained and go further with this search. Despite a lot of time and effort I was not able to find any information on Burchmon Asberry (besides the 1920 census) the man my father may have derived his name from.

GENERATION I	II	III	IV
Descendants.			
of Isaac Asbury, Sr.			
Of Virginia			

GENERATION I	II	III	IV
Isaac Asbury, Sr. 1820-	William Asberry, Sr 1841-1910	William Jr 1860-1935	Doretha 1900-1960
& Julia 1820-	Isaac 1844-1950	George 1881-	Hattie Beatrice
1902-1975	Louis George 1846-1918		William III 1907-1955
			Katie 1910-?
			Herman 1914-1989
			Ruth 1916-1939
			Isaac 1917-1994
			Thelma 1919-1984
			Douglas 1921-1973
			Ila 1904-
			Gertrude 1906-
			Clarence 1901-
			Wilma 1903-
			Leona 1904-
			George, Jr. 1907-
			Theola 1908-
			Edna 1913-
			Roland 1914-
			Burchmon 1915-
			Velma 1917-

My grandmother, Hattie Beatrice Asberry Taylor (1902-1975).

My great uncle, Herman Asberry, Sr. (1914-1989).

JONES/NETTERVILLE

Nancy Johns (aka Nancy Jones is truly the matriarch of the family. She will forever hold title of the first generation. Nancy Jones is my great great great grandmother. She was born in 1815, Liberty, Bedford County, Virginia. Nancy's father and mother's names and birthplaces are unknown. Perhaps her mother and father are descendent from Africa. One of my first questions was how did she obtained the surname of "Johns". History often tells us that slaves often took the name of the slaveholder. It is possible her slaveholder was named "John" and she used it as a surname, and later changed the spelling to "Jones". One such immigrant, John Henderson Gay, was of English and French descendent, and a branch of the family descending from Pocahontas. John Henderson Gay was also born in Virginia. His son, Edward James Gay was born about 1816, in Liberty, Bedford County, Virginia. John Henderson was married to Sophia Mitchell. My great great great grandmother, Nancy Johns names one of her daughters Sophia Johns (my great great grandmother). Coincidence or just confusing that the name is similar to the European gays? My great great grandmother, Sophia would later marry Anthony Gay. I would later discover that Anthony and Sophia Gay would give their children names similar to that of the European John Henderson Gay family used, i.e., John Gay and Edward James Gay. Oral interviews reports that great great grandfather Anthony Gay, was mixed with Indian. This might be another factor connecting my Gay ancestors to the European Gay family, who had a branch of the family descending from Pocahontas.

As stated above, Nancy was born in 1815. Changes in Black life grew after The War of 1812. Black Marylanders and Virginians (free and enslaved) were uprooted in a second Middle Passage and scattered throughout the United States. The Industrial Revolution created a great need for cotton. Between 1820 and 1860, to meet the growing demands of sugar and cotton, slaveholders developed an active domestic slave trade to move slaves to the South. Men, women and children marched South in large groups called coffles, covering on foot twenty-five to thirty miles a day. In 1860 nearly all adult Mississippi slaves had been either forced migrants to that state, or first generation Mississippi-born. On a small farm, or large plantation, most worked as farm laborers. In addition to farm laborer, other jobs included refining sugar, cooks, butlers, carpentry, and domestic servants. Slave families were broken up. An example, A Virginia slave father could be sold or moved to Mississippi, leaving one family only to start a new one, never knowing what happened to the family he left behind in Virginia. Slaves could not predict when an owner would die and how his estate would be divided.

The 1870 census provided me with a lot of information on Nancy Johns. Census takers are called enumerators. These enumerators were given instructions on how to take censuses. I found the misspelling of names. Names were written by the way it sounded to the census taker, an example "Sarre" and "Jesse" may be the same person. The date of birth was sometimes estimated based on how old the person appeared to the census taker. In 1870, Nancy Jones was now living in Woodville, Wilkinson County Mississippi. Reportedly she had ten children, with six still living. Was the other four deceased or sold, never to be seen again? Brutal treatment at the hands of slaveholders threatened Black family life. They lived with the constant fear of being sold away from their loved ones with no chance of a reunion. This census lists only four out of six of Nancy's "living" children - Sarre (dob 1852); Peyton (dob 1855); Armlia (dob 1858) and Sophia (dob 1860). A fifth, Burnetta Netterville Richardson (dob 1838) had left the home, and married. In the 1880 census, Nancy's household members were her daughter Sophia and two grandchildren – William Gay and Patey Jones. Nancy Jones died in Artonish, Wilkinson County, Mississippi on September 15, 1913. She died of a heart attack. She is buried in Deer Park Cemetery which is located on the border of Louisiana and Mississippi. I would have loved to have met Nancy (Johns) Jones, she probably seen and experienced a lot of hardship with a lot of stories to tell about her life journey.

Burnetta Netterville Richardson (dob 1838) is Nancy Jones first known child. The 1880 census lists Burnetta's race as a mulatto, an individual of mixed European and African ancestry. A Netterville Family Genealogy Report I found began with a William Netterville, Sr. (dob

December 2, 1736) who was born in Dowth, Meath, Ireland and died in Charleston, South Carolina. William Netterville was one of many Europeans who boarded a ship to the new nation. William's sons were John (dob 1763); William (dob 1765); Thomas (dob 1773); Charles (dob 1775) ; Jeremiah (dob 1777) and Jesse Netterville (dob 1780). This report along with the 1850 census shows that all of William's sons had moved from Charleston, South Carolina to Woodville, Wilkinson County, Mississippi. Burnetta had one known son with her husband, Sam Richardson and two daughters born earlier, Amanda Jones (dob 1869) and Mimah Kellogg (dob 1864). At sixteen years old, Mimah had a one year old, Lizzie Gay. Lizzie is believed to be the daughter of Anthony Gay, who also fathered Sophia's one year old, William Gay. In relationship, Sophia is Mimah's aunt. Burnetta died April 19, 1917 of pneumonia. Sophia Jones/Taylor (dob 1860) is believed to be Nancy Jones last born. She is my great great grandmother. The surname "Taylor" remains a mystery as to how it was derived. The name "Taylor" appears on Sophia's death certificate as her maiden name. The informant providing this information on the death certificate was her daughter, Annie Gay Taylor. Annie married my paternal great uncle, Isreal Taylor. In researching, I was able to see the 1880 census showing Sophia Taylor living in Brandon, Rankin County, Mississippi. A possible explanation for Sophia appearing in two households could mean that perhaps she was "visiting" the home in Rankin County at the time the census was taken. The "Head of Household" was an Isaac Taylor (dob 1800) born in Virginia. Sophia's mother, Nancy was also born in Virginia. The "relationship" to Sophia was listed as great grandfather. As early as 1837, Rankin County had a population of 3,255 free whites and 1,956 slaves. It is one of the oldest settlements, with the county seat at Brandon, named for Governor Gerald C. Brandon. Brandon, Rankin County, Mississippi is not too far from Plaquemine, Louisiana less than a hundred miles which is the home of my "Taylor" family. Could there be a connection between Isaac Taylor of Rankin County and Isreal, Isaiah and Armstead Taylor of Plaquemine, Iberville Parish, Louisiana? Could this be a connection? Could Sophia Taylor Gay be twice related to me like her daughter Annie Gay Taylor, on both my maternal and paternal sides of the family? Slaves were usually named by their owner. Male slaves appeared to use the surname of the owner as their surname whereas female slaves may have used the slaveholder first name as their surname, i.e. Johns/Jones.

The 1910 census shows Sophia Gay living in West Feliciana, Louisiana. Also, I found several of my Veal family ancestors living in West Feliciana. In Sophia's household were her daughters Annie Gay, who was eighteen years old and Clara Gay who was nine years old. The 1910 census shows that Sophia and Anthony are divorced. The household members are her daughter, Lucille Gay and her three grandchildren, Alma Swaine (dob 1905), Helen Weathers (dob 1907) my grandmother; and Clyde Weathers (dob 1909). Oral interviews reports that Lucille passed away around 1912 and 1914, when Clyde was about three years old. Unfortunately, I was told that Mississippi did not start keeping death records until after 1915. Lucille's cause of death is unknown. It is reported that there was an epidemic in 1913 which included influenza and smallpox. The epidemic was declared over by December 1913, although the last case was only notified in April 1914. No other influenza pandemic has been so deadly and no one knows why it was so lethal. This epidemic occurred in the wake of World War I, when the movement of large numbers of troops by sea and rail greatly facilitated the spread of the infection. The 1913 smallpox epidemic provides information on how this outbreak occurred. Could my great grandmother, Lucille Gay been one of the casualties of this pandemic outbreak? There were also 1920 and 1940 census records available on Sophie Gay who died in 1947.

GENERATION I	II	III	IV

DESCENDANTS
OF NANCY JOHNS
OF VIRGINIA

Nancy Johns (Jones) 1815-1913	Burnetta 1838-1917	Mimah Kellogg 1864-	
Jesse Netterville 1816-1892	Sarre 1852	Amanda Jones 1869-	
	Peyton 1855-	Sam Richardson 1870-	
	Armlia 1858-		
	Sophie 1862-1947	Alice Taylor 1878-	
	+ 5 other children	Patey Jones 1877-	
		William Gay 1879- 1946	Dr. Jacob A. Gay 1902-1975
		Annie Gay 1881-1954	
		Edward James Gay 1884-1966	
		Clara Gay 1885-1968	Lucille Scott 1913-1946
		Lucille Gay 1886-1911	Alma Swaine 1905-2000
			Helen Weathers 1907-1975
			Clyde Gay 1909-1976

JOHNS (CONT)

V	VI	VII	VIII
Gwendolyn 1939-	Shekita 1960-		
Clara 1941-	Andrew-		
Clarence 1943	Leander 1964-		
Celeste Lucille 1944	Meshone 1969-		
Henrietta 1946	Don 1961-		
Ora Lois 1924-	Antonio 1963-		
Rachel 1926-	Millette 1965		
Morell 1929-1998	Arndrill 1969-		
	Michelle- 1966		
	Latroya- 1979		
	Corey- 1971		
	Valencia- 1982		
	Barbara Jean 1948-1989	Demetria 1967-	Shaquille 1993-
	Patricia Ann 1949-	Bridgette 1979-	
	Brenda Joyce 1952	Tracie 1968-	Taron 1987-
	Deidre 1949-2004	William, Jr. 1973-2011	Jayden 2004-
	Desma 1966-	Dawn 1978-	Malia 2007-
		Taylor 1983-	Amira 2009-
		Sharnee 1963	Cameron
		Damien 1976-	Brenden
		Brandon 1984-	Amir
			Brenay

Nancy Johns (Jones) 1815-1913

Nancy Johns (Jones) 1815-1913 PICTURE NOT SHOWN

Sophie Taylor Gay 1862-1947

Lucille Gay 1886-1911

Helen Weathers 1907-1975

Morell Peterson Taylor 1929-1998

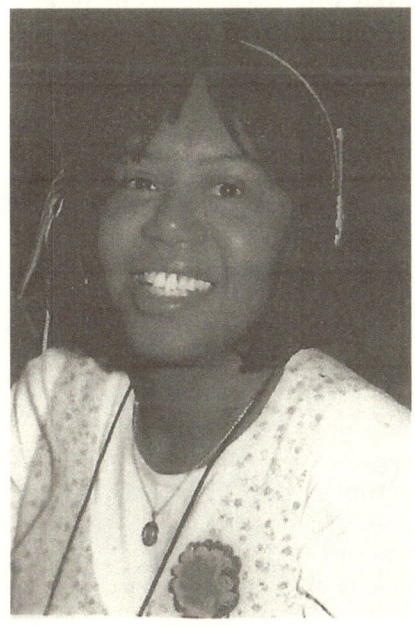

Patricia Ann Taylor-Mopkins 1949 –

Edward James Gay with his mother, Sophie and his nieces and nephews. My grandmother Helen Weathers is sitting in front. She was about six years old. Oicture was taken about 1912.

Entering Woodville, Wilkinson County, Mississippi.

A family portrait taken about 1920.

My great great uncle and his wife, Patsy. The little
boy is my grandmother's brother, Clyde Weathers
Gay. Picture was taken about 1915.

My great great grandmother Sophie Gay's nieces, Annette Wallace and Sophie Philips. The picture probable was taken around 1920. They were born about 1895 and 1898.

GENEALOGY, ETHNICITY AND DNA

Africans that were brought to this Great Nation and enslaved came from many regions of Africa. This may account for the difference in the physical characteristics of African American descendent. In my travels to Africa from 1998-2000, I had the opportunity to see African people of various regions. This included Dakar, Senegal and Accra, Ghana; The Gambia; Cotonou, Benin; Cape Town, Johannesburg, Pretoria and Soweto, South Africa; Nairobi, Kenya; Tanzania; Addis Ababa, Ethiopia and Harare, Zimbabwe. I knew that it would be highly unlikely that I could ever connect my ancestry to a specific village in Africa.

In April 2014, I took the Ancestry/DNA test. In my research, I learned that DNA is a great technology that is useful in determining one's African background. Ethnicity Genealogy Testing estimates are determined by comparing the DNA of other people who are native to a region. There is confidence that the representatives has a long history (hundreds of years) in that region. The DNA is then compared to the participant to the DNA in the reference panel to see which region the participant is most like. An estimate is calculated for each ethnicity region, using randomly selected portions of the participant. My DNA Ethnicity results were 87% - broken down by regions were the following: Cameroon/Congo 37%; Ivory Coast/Ghana 18%; Mali 16%; Benin/Togo 6%; Nigeria 4%; Senegal 1%; Africa South-Central Hunger-Gatherars 3%; America – Native American 1%; Asia 1%; Europe 9%; Ireland 4%; and Great Britain 2%.

My Ancestry DNA Ethnicity Estimate: Cameroon/Congo   37%; Ivory Coast/Ghana   18%;
Mali 16%;   Benin/Togo   6%;   Nigeria   4%;   Senegal   1%.

My Ancestry DNA Ethnicity Estimate: Cameroon/Congo 37%; Ivory Coast/Ghana 18%, Mali 16%; Benin/Togo 6%; Nigeria 4%; Senegal 1%

My DNA results are 37% Congo Region. Could my Asberry ancestors have descended from the Bambuto tribe, a tribe that was found living in the Congo Region with having a link to the Pygmy tribes. My paternal grandmother, Hattie Beatrice (dob 1902) was approximately 4'11. In the Asberry section I discuss that was one of the Asberry traits is being short in stature. In my research, I found that the earliest inhabitants of the Congo Region were the Bamuti people. The Bambuti were linked to Pygmy tribes, which were later replaced by the Bantu tribe. The main Bantu tribe living in the region was the Kongo, also known as Bokongo. The Bokongo, established weak and unstable kingdoms along the mouth, north and south of the Congo River. The Portuguese located the Congo River in 1482, where commerce was carried on with the tribes, especially the slave trade. The Congo is located in West Central Africa. It borders Gabon, Cameroon, The Central African republic, The Democratic Republic of the Congo,

Angola, with a short stretch of coast on the South Atlantic. It is about three times the size of Pennsylvania. In the 16th and 17th centuries British, Dutch, Portuguese and French merchants engaged in slave trade through Kongo intermediaries. Also in 1482, Portuguese navigator Diago Cao was the first European to visit the Congo and set up ties with the King of Kongo. It is reported that Portuguese imperialism along with the slave trade helped to destroy the tribes of the Bantu people.

A Congolese Woman

Myself

Look closely, do you see any similarities – the smile, structure of the nose cheek, eyebrow? My ancestry DNA ethnicity estimate was 37% Congolese.

EPILOGUE

This book focuses most on descendent of my family from the periods of 1800-1900. A family history was then built on branches of each family. Like most Black Americans, my ancestors were no different. From the time they left their homeland (Africa), they faced struggles, hardships and torture, trying to adjust and survive in the new nation. It is most likely that my ancestors came from West Africa. However, because no records were kept this information will never be substantiated. In some states, no official birth or death records of Black Americans until after 1912. Prior to this time, the federal census records were used as an official record which might not always be accurate. My presence on some of the busiest forts in West Africa where slaves were jailed in dungeons/cells until deported was a phenomenal experience. These forts were off the coast of Ghana, Senegal and Benin.

In the new nation, Africans began producing children. They were now called African Americans, amongst other derogatory names throughout the years. They were seen and counted as less than a person, receiving inhuman treatment. They were not allowed to vote, name their children, denied an education, separated families, etc. This journey allowed me to pause and reflect on what it must have been like for African Americans living during this period. My research made it more enlightening than reading history books or another author's work because it was more personal, it was my ancestors. The census records and other official documents, pictures of ancestors, visiting gravesites contributed to this reality. This reflection makes one appreciate more the freedom and pursuit of being happy that this country is built upon by our founding fathers. I can appreciate those groups who came before us, because of their struggles we now have an equal opportunity and can live a better life.

Lastly, one of the most interesting and exhausting part of this research was the complexity of how names were derived, given and repeated, from generation to generation. After the civil war, African

American appeared to name their children after their father, mother, brother, sister or other family member. There were so many Roberts in the Veal family and Williams in the Taylor and Asberry family that I was only able to keep track by their birth year. A tree has many branches from which a twig is sprout. It was impossible for me to list in this book the names (twigs) of all within each branch. For those who are not named hopefully this book may help you find from which branch you descended and continue where I left off. For those whose ancestors that were slaveholders and find it difficult to admit, be embarrassed or even deny that their ancestors caused this group of people such pain, the past is the past. It cannot be changed. But we all can say **NEVER AGAIN !!!**

SPECIAL CONCLUSION

It is my deepest regret to say that my wonderful and beautiful sister, Barbara Jean Taylor Risin Ivory is no longer with us. She passed away April 14, 1989. An angel has gone home. She left a void in my heart and in her family. Thank you God for the forty-one years you blessed us with her.

Patricia Ann Taylor

APPENDIX A

1880 United States Federal Census, Wilkinson County, Mississippi

Loc.	Household	Color	Age	Sex	Occupation	Place of Birth		
						Self	Fa	Mo
580-593	Gay, Mary	B	44	F	Farm Hand	MD	MD	MD
	-----, Anthony	B	20	M	Farm Hand	MS	VA	MD
	Veal, Ollie	B	22	F	Farm Hand	MS	MS	MS
581-594	Richardson, Charlie	Mu	48	M	Farm Hand	MS	MS	KY
	---------, Burnetta	Mu	40	F	Farm Hand	MS	MS	MS
	Jones, Amanda	B	11	F		MS	MS	MS
	Kellogg, Mimah	Mu	16	F	Farm Hand	MS	MS	MS
	Richardson, Sam	Mu	10	M		MS	MS	MS
	Hall, Willie	B	4	M		MS	MS	MS
	Gay, Lizzie	B	1	F		MS	MS	MS
582-596	Jones, Nancy	B	65	F	Farm Hand	MS	----	-----
	Taylor, Sophie	B	20	F	Farm Hand	MS	------	MS
	Gay, William	B	1	M		MS	MS	MS
	Jones, Patey	Mu	3	M		MS	MS	MS
583-596	Veal, Robert	B	51	M	Farm Hand	MS	MS	MS
	----, Virginia	Mu	31	F	Farm Hand	MS	MS	MS
	----, Richmond	B	16	M	Farm Hand	MS	MS	MS
	----, Jim	B	10	M		MS	MS	MS
	----, Tamar	B	8	F		MS	MS	MS
	----, Emily	B	6	F		MS	MS	MS

1880 United States Federal Census showing my great great great great grandmother, Nancy Johns (Jones). This page also depicts

other family members that lived in the community (The Gays, Veals and Bernetta Netterville Richardson and family). Nancy had 10 children. Source: 1880 U. S. Federal Census, Wilkinson County, Woodville, Mississippi, enumerated June 29, 1880, digital image. Ancestry.com http://www.ancestry.com (accessed August 11, 2009).

APPENDIX B

1900 United States Federal Census, Wilkinson County, Miss.

Loc.	Household	Color	Date of Birth	nativity			Occupation
				Self	Fa	Mo	
132-132	Veal, Isom	B	May 1853	MS	MS	MS	Farmer
135-135	Anderson, Maria	B	May 1810	Africa	Africa	Africa	Too old to work
139-139	Veal, Preston	B	August 1853	MS	TN	MS	Farmer
	----Margaret	B	Sept 1857	MS	MS	MS	Farm Laborer
	----William	B	August 1886	MS	MS	MS	at school
	Wright, Stewart	B	June 1888	MS	MS	MS	at school
141-141	Veal, Duncan	B	March 1835	MS	MS	MS	Farmer
	----- Mary	B	July 1850	MS	KY	MD	Farm Laborer

Throughout my entire research, Maria Anderson was the only person I came across who shown both her and her parents as a native from AFRICA. She is believed to be the widow of Robert Veal (1807-1895).

Source: 1900 United States Federal Census, Wilkinson County, Woodville, Mississippi, enumerated June 13, 1900, digital image. Ancestry.com http://www.ancestry.com (accessed March 7, 2013).

APPENDIX C

1880 United States Federal Census, Wilkinson County, Woodville, Mississippi

Loc.	Households	Color	Age	Sex	Occ.	Place of Birth		
						Self	Fa	Mo
333-364	Veal, William	B	76	M	House Servant	TN	TN	TN
	------, Mary	B	68	F	Keeping House	MD	MD	MD
334-365	Veal, Preston	B	27	M	Farm Laborer	MS	TN	MS
-	-----, Margaret	B	22	F	Farm Laborer	MS	MS	VA
332-363	Veal, Duncan	B	42	M	Farmer	MS	TN	MS
	------Mary	B	31	F	Keeping House	MS	MS	MS
	------Azarene	B	14	F	Farm Laborer	MS	MS	MS
	----- Milly	B	13	F	Farm Laborer	MS	MS	MS
	------Nannie	B	9	F	at school	MS	MS	MS
	------Norah	B	9	F	at school	MS	MS	MS

Source: 1880 United States Federal Census, Wilkinson County, Woodville, Mississippi, enumerated June 1880, digital image. Ancestry. com http://www.ancestry.com (accessed December 27, 2010)

APPENDIX D

1870 United States Federal Census: Iberville Parish, State of Louisiana

Loc.	Households	Age	Sex	C	Occ.	Value of Real Estate/Personal	Place of Birth
51-64	Gay, Edward James	53	M	W	Merchant	$700,000/$60000	Virginia
	------, Lavinia	47	F	W	Keeping House		Tennessee

Source: 1870 United States Federal Census, Schedule 1, enumeration district, eighth ward, Iberville Parish, State of Louisiana, digital image. Ancestry.com. http://www.ancestry.com (accessed May 13, 2010).

APPENDIX E

1880 United States Federal Census, Iberville Parish, Louisiana

Loc.	Household	Color	Age	Sex	Occupation	Place of Birth		
	Self	Fa	Mo					
481-5878	Taylor, Isreal	B	42	M	Laborer	LA	LA	LA
	------, Effie	B	25	F	Keeping house	NC	NC	NC
	-------, Charles	B	15	M	Laborer	LA	LA	LA
	Cox, William	B	13	M	Laborer	LA	LA	LA
482-588	Taylor, William	B	23	M	Laborer	LA	LA	LA
	-------, Dora	B	24	F	Keeping house	LA	LA	LA
	------, Elvira	B	2	F		LA	LA	LA
	-------, William	B	1	M		LA	LA	LA
487-397	Martin, William	B	70	M	Laborer	VA	VA	VA
	--------, Serena	B	60	F	Keeping House	VA	VA	VA
492-603	Martin, Richard	B	42	M	Laborer	LA	MD	MD
	--------, Mary	B	26	F	Keeping House	LA	MD	MD

Source: 1880 United States Federal Census, Iberville, Plaquemine, Louisiana, enumerated June 1880, digital image. Ancestry.com http://www.ancestry.com (accessed August 11, 2009.

APPENDIX F

SCHEDULE 1 – Free Inhabitant, Petersburg, Virginia, July 1860

Location	Households	Color	Age	Sex	Occupation	Place of Birth
1769-1730	Patsey Martin	B	49	F	Washwoman	Virginia

The 1860 United States Federal Census showing my great great great grandmother, who was born about 1811 and living in Petersburg, Virginia. It was an independent city in Virginia located on the Appomattox River and 23 miles from Richmond, Virginia.

Source: 1860 United States Federal Census, Petersburg (Independent City) Virginia, Enumerated July 1860, digital image. Ancestry. com. http:www.ancestry.com (accessed December 16, 2009).

APPENDIX G

1870 United States Federal Census, Iberville Parish, Louisiana

Loc.	Household	Color	Age	Sex	Occupation	Place of Birth
108-137	Martin, Albert	B	33	M	Farm Laborer	LA
	------, Elsy	B	27	F	Keeping House	LA
	------, Isaac	B	10	M		LA
	----, Kitto	B	8	M		LA
	------, Adam	B	6	M		LA
	------, William	B	5	M		LA
	------, Nancy	B	3	F		LA
	, Albert Jr.	B	1	M		LA
109-138	Martin, Richard	B	30	M	Farm Laborer	LA
	---, Charlotte	B	28	F	Keeping House	LA
	------, Dora	B	10	F		LA
	------, Julia	B	8	F		LA
	------, Richard Jr.	B	6	M		LA
	------, Sirrus	B	4	M		LA
141-51	Martin, Isaac	B	58	M	Farm Laborer	MD
	-------, Patsey	B	55	F	Keeping House	VA
	------, Cornelius	B	18	M	at home	LA
	------,Richard	B	13	M	at home	LA
	-------, William	B	11	M	at home	LA
142-52	Martin, George	B	30	M	Farm Laborer	LA
	------, Clara	B	25	F	Keeping House	LA
	------, Estelle	B	10	F		LA
	------, Henry	B	8	M		LA
	------, Wade	B	4	M		LA
	------, Sarah	B	1	F		LA

BIBLIOGRAPHY

What follows is not intended as a comprehensive bibliography on slavery or of a specific aspect of that institution. What is provided is a list of documents, federal records and census materials from which this work was drawn, in addition to secondary sources, books, articles that were consulted.

Primary Sources

Documents

Louisiana State, Secretary of State, Division of Archives, Records and Management and History, P.O. Box 94125, Baton Rouge, Louisiana 70804-9125.

Federal Records – Social Security Death Index, Land Records, Military Records (National Archives – include service records, U.S. Wars, pension applications and death records of pensioners.

Religious Records – Marriage; Death and Burial Records.

Population Schedule of the Eighth Census of the United States, 1850.

Population Schedule of the Ninth Census of the United States, 1860.

Population Schedule of the Tenth Census of the United States, 1870.

Population Schedule of the Eleventh Census of the United States, 1880.

Population Schedules of the Twelve Census United States, 1900.

Population Schedule of the Thirteenth Census of the United States, 1910.

Population Schedule of the fourteenth Census of the United States, 1920.

Population Schedule of the fifteenth Census of the United States, 1930.

Population Schedule of the Sixteenth Census of the United States, 1940.

Secondary Sources

Articles

"The Burning of Bowling Green", (excerpts from) by Stella M. and James Pitts.

Edward James Gay, from Wikipedia, the free encyclopedia.

United States Colored Troops, from Wikipedia, the free encyclopedia.

"Life on a Southern Plantation, 1854" Eyewitness to History, eyewitnesstohistory.com.

John Harvey Kellogg, from Wikipedia, the free encyclopedia.

"Indian Tribes of Mississippi", trails.mdah.ns.gov/tribes.

Mississippi Slavery, rootsweb.com.

"African American in Slavery" Delta region, National Park Service, February 8, 2001 (1-4).

Sankofa's Plantation Database, rootsweb.com.

"A Pictorial History of the Mississippi Steamboating Era", Steamboating. com/steamboats 1861-1899.

Biographies of Presidents James Monroe, John Quincy Adams, Andrew Jackson, Martin Van Buren, William Henry Harrison, John Tyler, James Polk, Zachary Taylor and Theodore, whitehouse.gov/about presidents.

A letter to me, Reference #M75130 from Mississippi Department of Archives and History, P.O. Box 571, Jackson, Mississippi 39205-6964, stating no official birth records were kept by the state of Mississippi until November 1912. Prior to that time, census records can be used to determine the birth year.

Slavery in America, the reason we went to war "The American Civil War", Ronald W. McGranahan, 2004.

"Slavery in Maryland", Smithsonian Anacostia Community Museum.

West Feliciana Railroad, contributed from the 1980 Audubon Pilgrimage Booklet by the WFP Historical Society.

Wilkinson County, Mississippi 1860 slaveholders and 1870 African American, transcribed by Tom Blake, April 2001.

Frank B. Williams "Cypress Lumber King" by Anna C. Burns, Journal of Forest History, July 1980.

Jeffersoncountyms.org/cypressgrove.htm

"Which Presidents own Slaves", home.nas.com/lopresti/ps.

"Lieutenant General Richard Taylor (1826-1879)", usskidd.com/taylor.

BOOKS

Ball, Edward, Slaves In The Family, 1998.

Blockson, Charles., Black Genealogy, 1977.

Boubacar, Doro Ba, Senegal, 1998.

Boubacar, Joseph Ndiaye, Principle Curator of the Slave House of Goree-Island, The Slave House of Goree Island, Dakar-Senegal.

Campbell, Jr., Edward D. C. with Kym S. Rice, editors – Before Freedom Came "African-American Life in the Antebellum South, The museum of the Confederacy, Richmond and the University Press of Virginia, Charlottesville.

Collins, Gail, "William Henry Harrison", 2012.

Francis, Sandra, "Benjamin Harrison, Our Twenty-third President", 2009.

Diouf, Sylviane A., "Dreams of Africa in Alabama", 2007.

Gutman, Herbert, G., "The Black Family in Slavery and Freedom – 1750-1925", 1975.

Hembold, F. Wilbur, Tracing Your Ancestry, 1976.

Hurmence, Belinda, "When I Just Can Remember", 1989.

Latham, William, How To Find Your Family Roots, 1988.

Law, W Augustus and Virgil A. Clift, Encyclopedia of Black America, 1981.

Maryland State Archives, A Guide to the History of Slavery in Maryland.

McLaurin, Melton A., "Celia, A Slave", 1991.

Northrup, Solomon, "Twelve Years A Slave": A Narrative of Solomon Northrup, a citizen of New York Kidnapped in Washington in 1841, and rescued in 1853 from a cotton plantation near Red River, Louisiana, 2007. Originally published in 1853.

Quidah, FIT edition, Cotonou, Republic of benin.

Steen, Johan B. and Esben Ridderwold, "The Masai people", 1993.

Still, William, "The Underground Railroad", 2005.

Taylor, Joe Gray -"Negro Slavery in Louisiana", 1963.

Taylor, Joe Gray – Louisiana, a History "Moonlight, Magnolias, Moneymaking and Politics, 1984.

Thomas, Velma Maia – Lest we Forget "The Passage from Africa to Slavery and Emancipation, 1997.

Tomkinson, Michael, "Gambia", 2000.

Underground Railroad, Handbook 156, National Park Services, U. S. Department of Interior, Washington D. C.

Woodson, Carter G. "The mind of the Negro as reflected in letters written during the crisis 1800-1860", 1926.

ACKNOWLEDEMENTS

So many people have stood by me during my journey. I am deeply grateful to all those who have supported me and offered their love, support and encouragement.

My daughter, Tracie Marie Denise Hawkins-Gaines always showed a deep interest in the family history. My daughter, Dawn Millette Mopkins, thank you for reading the manuscript over and over again helping me with the page layout and other parts of the manuscript despite your busy schedule J. My daughter, Taylor Ashley Jackson who assisted me in any way she could and inspired me with her positive attitude.

A special thanks to the skills of my team at AuthorHouse. I am very appreciative of your enthusiasm and support, the marketing team, the extraordinary sales force, all at AuthorHouse.

ABOUT THE AUTHOR   Patricia Taylor brings a unique point of view to this book. She has traveled to Africa, Asia, Europe and South America. Her travels to North, South, East and West Africa gives her the knowledge of the area, its people and history. Her travels to New York, Maryland, Virginia, North Carolina, South Carolina, Georgia, Louisiana and Mississippi takes the reader on a chilling journey of American History before Emancipation, when Union Troops arrived.

Taylor's grandparents were Louisiana sharecroppers. She was born in the small town of Plaquemine, Louisiana. Since the publishing of the book "Roots" by Alex Haley, she has had a strong interest on the arrival of Africans to America and their migration to the South.